MIMES ON MIMING

Bari Rolfe

Mimes on Miming

WRITINGS ON THE ART OF MIME

edited with historical notes by
BARI ROLFE

Panjandrum Books
Los Angeles   San Francisco

First Printing.

Cover design by Catherine Conner
Cover photo of Dimitri, clown: Courtesy of Dimitri

Library of Congress Cataloging in Publication Data

Main entry under Title:

Mimes on Miming.

  Bibliography: p.
  Includes index.
  1. Mime—Collected works. I. Rolfe, Bari.
PN2071.G4M5   792.3   79-21659
ISBN 0-915572-32-X
ISBN 0-915572-31-1 pbk.

Acknowledgments and permissions on page 225 constitute an extension of this copyright page.

Panjandrum Books
11321 Iowa Avenue, Suite 1
Los Angeles, Calif. 90025

Manufactured in the United States of America

I offer this book in memory
of two men
whose work has given me indescribable pleasure.

Charles Chaplin 1889–1977
Tristan Rémy 1897–1977

Acknowledgments

MY WARM APPRECIATION is offered to those friends and colleagues who have helped this work along, among them Marcel Marceau for his early encouragement, and John Towsen and Leslie Carr for reading the manuscript and making valuable suggestions. Leonard Pronko and Kathy Foley gave me sources on Asian theatre. Justine Van Gundy, Ruby Cohn and Helen Krich Chinoy were generous with interest and advice, and Antonin Hodek was good enough to make some translations from the Czech. The reference personnel at the University of California, Berkeley, library were most helpful, as was Russell Hartley of the Archives for the Performing Arts in San Francisco. My thanks to the holders of copyrights, too numerous to mention individually, who permitted the use of material either free of charge or at low fees, and whose generosity made this compilation possible. And my appreciation goes to my publisher Dennis Koran for his interest from the early stage of this manuscript and for his helpful editing as the book was brought to fruition.

Contents

Illustrations

Prologue

MIMES TALKING ABOUT mime? That's almost a contradiction in terms; have not the authors chosen the act over the word? Surprisingly, there is too much material available, rather than too little, and for every entry that a reader finds interesting, provocative, or delightful, my wistful comment is "Yes, and there are lots more that got away!"

My hope is that *all* theatre lovers will find this volume of interest. Many selections were made specifically with actors, dancers, clowns, directors, choreographers, historians, or film buffs in mind. Besides there are all those cross-overs: mimes who were/are also dancers, and who make films, who clown . . . . Happily for all, dividing lines have a way of wiggling away from the analytical pinpoint.

What is mime? Who is a mime? The impossibility of definitive answers is demonstrated in the entry "Meem, Mime, and Pantomime." There, readers will find conflicting opinions about these words. In ancient Greece and Rome a mime was a sketch or dialogue, as in Herodas' *The Mimes of Herodas* and Lucian's *Mimes of the Courtisans*. Actors who interpreted a given scene in gesture or dance, often with masks, were called pantomimes. In the Middle Ages and through the Renaissance the term dumb show was used for a play, or scene done in silence, using gestures. Later the same form was called pantomime, and in general this term has been used since then for silent performance, with variations. Many variations.

Pantomime has no coherent history, although traces of it can be observed over a period of almost three thousand years, according to Oto Bihalji-Merin in *Great Masks*. It probably is even older, for drama was born with humankind itself, and gesture was the first form of expression and social communication. Performing mime, we know, was already developed and varied when it appeared in early records, so there is no knowing how long it had already existed. But because early descriptions are meager, historians usually begin discussing theatrical mime with the Greeks and Romans.

Of course there was, and is, what might be called cultural mime or pantomime: imitative dances, sympathetic magic, fertility dances, religious ritual. This is a huge subject, much greater than the present one, and has been admirably dealt with elsewhere, although not necessarily under that term; it belongs to anthropology, sociology, and religion. The mime represented here is that of performers of a theatrical art composed and offered before audiences—mime as spectacle.

1

In addition to the writings of actual mime performers, which comprise the bulk of the book, I have included material published by teachers of mime, composers of mime sketches, critics, and historians when their works have struck me as being particularly important or enjoyable, especially for the early periods for which few writings are available. Unfortunately, some mimes are not represented because I could find no appropriate written material: Samy Molcho and Shai K. Ophir from Israel; Holland's Rob Van Reyn; Mata and Hari, Tony Montanaro and Claude Kipnis from the United States among them. With some exceptions, then, this anthology might serve as an historical survey of mimes up to the twentieth century, or to about 1950. For the immediate present, the hand of history has not yet written the names of the immortals, nor even of those who simply will be remembered in the future, who by virtue of talent, luck, or good public relations will weather the eroding process of time. The impossibility of including, or even mentioning, every present performer is obvious. Readers who are interested in finding many names can refer to the *Mime Directory* published by the International Mimes and Pantomimists, College of Visual & Performing Arts, Syracuse University, Syracuse, NY 13210; there can be found the great majority of contemporary mimes.

Through these essays we will follow the bright, seductive flute and drum down the historical path traced by pantomimes, comic players, clowns, jugglers, and acrobats, from ancient Greece and Rome, through the dim tunnel of medieval mumming, mystery and miracle plays and fairground booths, to the stylized, sophisticated players of Asian total theatre of dialogue, mime, dance, and song. Then we emerge into the sunlight of *commedia dell'arte* and the intermezzi of Elizabethan and Spanish Renaissance theatre. Still following the lure of the tambourine we see the tiny procession winding through English panto and French action-ballet; Pierrots and Charlots beckon us into the more familiar realm of music hall and circus; then to the beginning of the hundred-year-reign of French pantomime. We come finally to a smashing fanfare that opens the curtain on the dizzying, world-wide array of mime today—the clowns, silent comics, dancers, vaudevillians, surrealists, agit-prop, maskers; in TV, films, on the stages and in the streets—mimes all.

So, the many minds of many mimes, a feast by fools of every flavor. Wise fools, to be sure, in the ways that revealing gesture and audible silence made them wise.

Curtain-raiser

To Talk of Mime . . .
Dominique Bourquin

Mlle Bourquin is a young Swiss actress who also writes on theatre subjects. Taken from Mimes Suisses, Un Aperçu.

To TALK OF MIME, to give it a definition, almost an impossibility. To say, as does the dictionary, that it is the action of imitating is somewhat limited; to say that it is theatre without words is to reduce it to the state of a preliterate child; to say that it is the art of picking flowers without flowers, of climbing stairs without steps, is to confine it to a game of riddles. To say—they say so many things about mime.

What is certain is that the word "mime" has changed its meaning over the course of time. At its outset a silent drama ridiculing the faults of contemporary society, it found words and extended itself to all stages: farce, satire, clowning. Stressing satire, mime fixed on several types such as Merchant, Judge, etc. Then it again lost use of the word for, little appreciated by those who pay the expenses, it became dangerous and liable to sanctions.

In time, the mime became illusionist, clown, wandering minstrel, acrobat, reciter of poems, and passed somehow through the traps laid by the authorities. He came a cropper a bit more harshly in the seventeenth century when confronted by a series of prohibitions which permitted him only to present some harmless acrobatics. Harlequins and Pierrots of all shades were compelled to fight for survival during the two following centuries. Admittedly the enemy was a real adversary, nothing less than the tragic theatre born in the age of Louis XIV that tried with all its power to render itself safe from rivalry.

But little by little, piece by piece, success aiding its efforts, mime gained ground. It would soon have its theatres and its stars. The now numerous public would come to applaud its mimics, rope-dancers, and acrobats. Under the Restoration the Harlequinade pantomime reached its height. But soon the appearance of vaudeville delivered it a new blow and forced it to convert again; thus came about the emergence of realistic mimed plays by mainly tragic authors. The principal character of this particular genre was Pierrot. He lived for almost a century, since it was only in 1927 that the last true Pierrots, Théodore Thalès and Séverin, bade their farewells.

The disappearance of Pierrot coincided in effect with the beginnings
of contemporary mime. This new birth was owed, certainly, to Etienne
Decroux who, after the second World War, perfected a severe discipline that he called "mime corporel." At no other time was mime so
intrinsically bound to the body, with the arms, hands and face often
functioning simply as resonators. "Mime corporel" involved an in-
tense training that aimed at purifying movement, to live it in its
entirety, with no external flourish. If Decroux has not won considerable success in his presentations, he remains nevertheless a great
master of the technique of mime. Certainly, the birth of two great
talents was due largely to his teaching: Jean-Louis Barrault, whose
training later took him to the theatre and a well-known career, and
Marcel Marceau. The latter devotes himself to what is called "style
pantomimes." He invented the character of Bip, having him exercise
all kinds of occupations and embark on numerous adventures. His
talent and authority have won him such a success that the public
itself has come to confuse him with the art he practices. "Mime?
Why, it's Marceau!" one often hears. By virtue of his genius he has
succeeded in crystallizing around himself the opinion of a great many
people who have set him up as a reference, a model. "Whatever does
not resemble Marceau, it's not mime!" This fixation is certainly
excessive. It is as though one excluded implicitly all forms of modern
dance in favor of only classical dance.

Indeed, the mime of today has exploded the rigid constraints of
classicism and is developing several new tendencies. For example, in
deepening its search for physical and gestural techniques, it attempts
to discover the elementary, intrinsic forces of movement and of dy-
namics, which thus become the physical expression of a psychic
energy. Yves Lebreton, one of the best representatives of this tendency, said, "The actor is no longer the representation of a character
registered within the limits of particularism, but he becomes the
physical expression of the internal thought that impels him . . . each
muscular contraction or release is the reflection of an interior state.
At that point of deepest relation between the behavior and the intellect, the body and the thought are united in a single totality." The
mimes who participate in this starting point therefore abandon the
anecdote and the narrative, in favor of pure abstraction. This is not to
be confused with estheticism, which constitutes still another genre,
but it offers itself rather as the attempt to express the profound
reality of humankind without going through the reciting of a tale, that
is, with the least possible rational and cultural intermediaries between the expression and its motivation. However refined the technique may be, one can in a certain sense speak of raw expression,

without implying instinctive, passionate, or "animal." Rather than illustrating the particular, this starting point aims at the totality of expressing the thought, feelings, and instincts of humankind.

Another tendency of today's mime seeks to free itself from the final vestiges of Pierrots that mainly continue to set up guessing games for the public, in a series of little sketches. While retaining the more or less realistic narrative and anecdote, these mimes are discarding their makeup, their mask, and their traditional costume in order to find their own face. They are no longer afraid to surround themselves with real objects, to use sounds and music, and even at times to pronounce a few words. If some of them use masks, it is rather in this new perspective. The mask becomes an entirely separate element to play with, which transforms itself, becomes meaningful in itself. Thus, a new theatrical genre has seen the light of day. Is it mime? Is it theatre? The question has no meaning. What is certain is that it continues to search for a specific language of the body, and objects and sounds themselves have a value altogether different from that in spoken theatre. Body, objects, sounds strengthening each other, express themselves each one in its own language, perceptible only if they respect a certain "silence."

There, quickly sketched out, are two major trends, among others, of contemporary mime. To be sure, they are not separated, and permit of numerous combinations.

Do these remarks bring us any closer to the sought-for definition of mime? To say that it is the favored language of the body as expression of the mind, it's true but vague and incomplete! To say that it is marginal theatre where silence reveals the specific character of gesture is equally true, but how insufficient! To say that . . . they say so many things about mime!

Meem, Mime, and Pantomime
Bari Rolfe

M IME IS THAT STRANGE creature which all of us recognize when we
see it—or do we? And everyone agrees that it started 'way back
then, only what was it? The confusion and lack of agreement even
among practitioners is evident in the following collection of termi-
nology. To compound the confusion, some languages (German, Czech)
have no separate word for "mime"; it is all called "pantomime."
These words have changed their meanings without so much as a glance
at the definition-makers. Yet the urge for, the search for, definition
has never stopped. Any definition inevitably brings to mind its exceptions, and both of these words have continually changed over the
years. It is still tempting to try to separate whatever one means by
"mime," this fluid, flexible, sensitive art form, this kinesthetic way
of looking at the world, from dance or English panto or eurhythmics
or mimed ballads or . . . . Perhaps what is most important is that a
definition does not close creative doors, that it always follows the
artistic thrust and does not precede it to act as a formula or recipe.
Instead of definitions let us hope for less "What is it?" and more "How
does it stretch appreciation of movement and its effect?"

The changing, tantalizing Bird of Pantomime has skipped and flitted
its way throughout all countries for centuries, defying anyone to cage
it for long within a definition. Many have tried to put salt on its tail;
the Bird itself is confused and is heard asking quizzically, "Am I a
noun, a verb, or a fad?" as it gaily hops from perch to *perch*, scat-
tering joy with never a thought to the past or future.

*   *   *

The mimes say:

"Most of the Roman *mimes* were little comedies, libertine and lic-
entious, from the naturalistic school of Alexandria and were played
essentially in dialogue and without masks. The actors who interpreted
them, *mimologues*, had nothing in common with the *panto-mime*,
silent actor who carried the entire play on his shoulders, using up to
five masks for a play—a gesture virtuoso" (Yves Lorelle).

Rosamond Gilder describes Greek *mimes* as marketplace entertainers, very much like cabaret performers of today; they engaged in satiric, untrammeled antics. Roman *mime* was similar, using dance,

music, gymnastics, and clowning. In contrast, the Roman *panto-mimist* was an actor and dancer in one, holding the stage alone and interpreting, through gesture, movement, attitude and costume, a whole drama, in which he assumed successively all the roles required.

"By the word *dance*, as one will see, I do not at all mean the art of moving to a measured beat, of gracefully delineating cadenced steps. This word throughout the course of this work means none other than the art of gesture" (François l'Aulnaye). "*Pantomime*, in antiquity was a play, basically imitative. Besides the silent action, the *panto-mime* included the text describing the events, and the musical accompaniment" (Jean Dorcy).

"In the mid-eighteenth century, Noverre created *heroic pantomime*. In France was born the *pantomime* of the Funambules, the play spoken, played, and danced, from the *commedia dell'arte*. Today *pantomime* is a term of little content, often employed without relevance to designate a play without text and without dance" (Jean Dorcy).

"*Pantomime* is a language of action or dumb show" (Charles Aubert). "Modern *pantomime* is the art of expressing sentiments, while the *pantomime* known as 'classic' is the means of translating words by use of gesture" (Georges Wague). "The word *mime* represents the actor who expresses himself in gesture, *pantomime* refers to the mimed play. One ought to call the silent actor a *pantomime*, but I call myself a *mime*" (Séverin).

"Gesture is a movement having a definite word or occupational significance" (Irene Mawer). Gertrude Pickersgill uses the term *word-mime* for *pantomime*. "*Pantomime* is generally used to mean the telling of a story or incident without the use of words. It is body action to reveal thought; it is condensed dramatic action" (T. E. Pardoe).

"The art of the stage developed from *mime*, which is the representation of inner movements by visible outer motions. A *mime* often transmits to the spectator what kind of an inner struggle his character is going through solely by his body, carriage, or posture, without perceptible movement or sound" (Rudolf Laban).

For Jean-Louis Barrault, *mime* is the art of silence. Closely following is Antonin Artaud's *direct pantomime*, where gestures represent ideas, attitudes of mind or aspects of nature, all in an effective, concrete manner, instead of representing words or sentences. Jacques Lecoq defines *pantomime* as a gesture substituting for a word (you, me, swim, etc.) and *mime* as communication when words do not exist, are not needed. And for Marcel Marceau *mime* is the physical identification with the elements which surround us, the art of gesture and attitude. A number of contemporary French mimes share the same general concepts, that *pantomime* is the substitution for a word, *mime* is silent and nonliterary.

Angna Enters offers that *mime* is communication by means of gesture symbols: gesture, smile, glance, reflective thought, or physical action. She adds a new term: *mimesis* is the representation of reality by means of actions, with or without words. *Pantomime*, says Paul Curtis, is the art of creating the illusion of reality by dealing with imaginary objects or situations; *mime* is the art of acting silently through various kinds of theatrical movement. R. G. Davis: *Mime* is the motivating of external movement from an internal source. And Leonard Pitt: *Pantomime* is the use of object illusions, and *mime* is a physical language of emotional expression. Others too have separated the two according to whether objects are imaginary (pantomime) or real (mime).

Carlo Mazzone-Clementi: *Mime* is a preliterary condition; definitely the alphabet was invented by illiterates, probably mimes.

*   *   *

These very sketchy references are meant to display the wide range of nonagreement. Almost the only aspect of the subject on which everyone agrees is that the forms involve movement. But immobility is also a form of movement! So there we are.

Meem! Oh, that's simply the French pronunciation for the word *mime*.

Figure 1. Roman mimes.

I. Mime in Greece and Rome

Barbarian, to the Mime: Tho' you have but one Body, you have many souls.

> —Lucian

Roscious proved to Cicero that by his employment of gesture and dumb show he could move the spectators in the judgment of the arbiters, as much or more than Cicero had been able to by his eloquent orations.

. . . the Rope-dancers drew all the spectators from my Play . . .

> —Terence

*On every side his active Body plies
In various Whirls, and strikes our ravish'd Eyes;
His Head, his Feet, and Busy Fingers make
A dumb Orator, and we see him speak.*

> —Nonnus

MIME CAME TO GREECE from several sources. From Egypt came mystery plays and imitative dances, which mingled with mask dances and dithyrambs of Dionysus. Dorian mimes arrived in the fifth century B.C. from Megara, on the Corinthian isthmus, an area that was invaded by the Dorians.

The Etruscan mimes were in Rome, to which they had been summoned because of their "international"—that is, Mediterranean—reputation in the fourth century B.C. They were farcical players, actors who "danced to the flute in the Tuscan manner." With their songs, dances, declamations and gross farces they greatly influenced Roman theatre. According to designs on Etruscan tombs, they also played at funerary rites with elegance and grace, enacting myths and legends with highly codified gestures. Another, perhaps greater influence on Roman theatre were the Atellan mimes from southern Italy, around Naples, widely known for their farces. Their contributions included stock characters, short spoken plays on themes of everyday life, and the use of song, improvisation, and satire. Other entertainers accompanied the players: acrobats, musicians, charlatans, funambuli (rope walkers), jugglers, magicians, stilt walkers, and animal acts. Allardyce Nicoll summarizes it in *Masks, Mimes and Miracles* as a vast dramatic movement, arising in or around Megara, spreading south to Egypt and west to Italy, and retaining always its major element, the depiction of real, everyday life (in contrast to tragic, heroic themes).

Origin of pantomime

A legend tracing the origin of Roman pantomime, as they called it, to an accident befalling Livius Andronicus in 240 B.C. is much repeated. According to the legend, the poet-actor, on declaiming his own verses, is said to have been so well liked by the public that too many performances caused his voice to fail; he then assigned a slave the task of speaking the lines while he enacted the expression of them. Pretty as the story is, it lacks conviction. Although history is tantalizingly obscure, there is mention of a dramatic form consisting of danced or acted stories accompanied by song or verse, from earlier periods. It had appeared in Sicily, was imported into Greece and thence to Rome in the third century B.C., according to Crowell's *Handbook of Classical Drama*, and undoubtedly originated in cult ritual. Boulenger de Rivery says, in *Recherches Historiques*, that in the fourth epoch (date uncertain) there occurred a separation between actors who spoke and actors who expressed the meaning and the emotion of the words. In

The Italian Comedy Duchartre describes Atellan farces as improvisations from scenarios, adding that it was frequently the custom for one actor to recite while another acted the story; acted plots, requiring no spoken text, were popular throughout the polyglot Roman Empire.

Nicoll tells us that pantomime existed alongside the acted mime farces. Pantomime denoted those performances in which a dancer danced/acted to an accompanying song or text given by a chorus or singer. The artist used various masks for the different characters, imitating all of them (*pantomime*). Sometimes the text was spoken or declaimed by players or *histriones*. Subjects were taken from myth or legend and treated seriously; when the pantomimes dealt with sensuous Dionysian themes they did not escape being called obscene.

Greek and Roman pantomime

In Greece the art of gesture was called *orchesis*. Aristotle speaks of *mimetic dances*. *Pyrrhic dances* were a sort of military pantomime, with blows and counterblows set to music, one combatant being overcome and the other singing his triumph. The *Ethologues*, "painters of manners," sought to demonstrate and inculcate moral lessons through pantomime. There were also light, farcical pieces, comic pieces honoring Bacchus, noble and tragic dance, and drunken, phallic farces.

The Romans brought the art of pantomime to great heights. Subjects ranged from serious treatment of myth and legend to farcical burlesques. They called it *saltation*, dancing, and to dance a tragedy was synonymous with acting a pantomime. These pantomimes often appeared between scenes of a written play as intermezzi, or as afterpieces. Women performed as dancers, singers, and pantomimists, only later coming under a churchly ban. The Romans valued highly the art of gesture, and the school of rhetoric for orators and politicians also graduated actors and mimes.

Attracted to this art of gesture were writers and philosophers, who called it a "marvelous art which makes the limbs speak when the tongue is silent." Seneca (55 B.C.–37/41 A.D.) found thoughtful ideas mixed in with their comedy. Cicero (106 B.C.–43 B.C.) admired the players for having a tongue at each finger's end. At the same time, they were berated by other critics for their obscenities in gesture.

Pylades was a freed Sicilian slave of Augustus, and was acclaimed for his serious, or tragic, style. His rival Bathyllus, also a freed slave from Alexandria, was equally famed for his comic style. Competition between them was strong enough to provoke their followers into sharp conflicts. The subjects of their plays were often drawn from mythology.

Political fortunes of the pantomimes seesawed from favor to banishment. Pylades was exiled by Augustus. Tiberius suppressed private shows. Caligula recalled the exiled players, then drove them out again. Domitian allowed only private performances. Trajan banished them, then brought them back. Nero the same. The players' fortunes ebbed and flowed with each emperor; traces are lost after about 520 A.D.

There was, however, at least one more well-known mime: Theodora (500–548) of Constantinople in the Eastern Roman Empire. Born into a circus family, she played in pantomimes, *tableaux vivants*, and comic mimes from her earliest years. Mischievous and audacious, she was highly popular with the polyglot public of the city. She was also of rare intelligence, beautiful, and enjoyed superior virtues—all qualities that enabled her to become a compassionate, wise ruler reigning jointly with her husband Justinian over Byzantium.

*   *   *

With the fall of the Roman Empire, Polymnia (or Polyhymnia), the Muse of Mime, wandered with the jugglers, jesters and acrobats who remained as popular as ever in both public and private performances, despite the repeated attempts by the church to outlaw them for their obscenities. Soon, however, Polymnia would be needed by the very same church for its mimed mystery scenes of religious drama, and for the processions and intermezzi of Renaissance theatre.

On Pantomime

Lucian

Lucian (c 120–200 A.D.) was a Greek writer, lawyer, and instructor of rhetoric. He wrote many dialogues on contemporary life and customs.

AND NOW I COME to the pantomime. What must be his qualifications? What his previous training? What his studies? What his subsidiary accomplishments? You will find that his is no easy profession, nor lightly to be undertaken; requiring as it does the highest standard of culture in all its branches, and involving a knowledge not of music only, but of rhythm and metre, and above all of your beloved philosophy, both natural and moral, the subtleties of dialectic alone being rejected as serving no useful purpose. Rhetoric, too, in so far as that art is concerned with the exposition of human character and human passions, claims a share of its attention. Nor can it dispense with the painter's and the sculptor's arts; in its close observance of the harmonious proportions that these teach, it is the equal of an Apelles or a Phidias. But above all Mnemosyne, and her daughter Polyhymnia, must be propitiated by an art that would remember all things. Like Chalches in Homer, the pantomime must know all "that is, that was, that shall be"; nothing must escape his ever ready memory. Faithfully to represent his subject, adequately to express his own conceptions, to make plain all that might be obscure—these are the first essentials for the pantomime, to whom no higher compliment could be paid than Thucydides's tribute to Pericles, who, he says, "could not only conceive a wise policy, but render it intelligible to his hearers"; the intelligibility, in the present case, depending on clearness of gesticulation.

For his materials, he must draw continually, as I have said, upon his unfailing memory of ancient story; and memory must be backed by taste and judgment. He must know the history of the world, from the time when it first emerged from Chaos down to the days of Egyptian Cleopatra.

Since it is his profession to imitate, and to show forth his subject by means of gesticulation, he, like the orators, must acquire lucidity; every scene must be intelligible without the aid of an interpreter; to borrow the expression of the Pythian oracle.

Dumb though he be, and speechless, he is heard by the spectator. According to the story, this was precisely the experience of the Cynic Demetrius. He had inveighed against Pantomime in just your own

14

terms. The pantomime, he said, was a mere appendage to flute and pipe and beating feet; he added nothing to the action; his gesticulations were aimless nonsense; there was no meaning in them; people were hoodwinked by the silken robes and handsome mask, by the fluting and piping and the fine voices, which served to set off what in itself was nothing. The leading pantomime of the day—this was in Nero's reign—was apparently a man of no mean intelligence; unsurpassed, in fact, in wideness of range and in grace of execution. Nothing, I think, could be more reasonable than the request he made of Demetrius, which was, to reserve his decision till he had witnessed his performance, which he undertook to go through without the assistance of flute or song. He was as good as his word. The time-beaters, the flutes, even the chorus, were ordered to preserve a strict silence; and the pantomime, left to his own resources, represented the loves of Ares and Aphrodite, the telltale Sun, the surrounding Gods, each in his turn, the blushes of Aphrodite, the embarrassment of Ares, his entreaties—in fact the whole story. Demetrius was ravished at the spectacle; nor could there be higher praise than that with which he rewarded the performer. "Man," he shrieked at the top of his voice, "this is not seeing, but hearing and seeing, both: 'tis as if your hands were tongues!"

And before we leave Nero's times, I must tell you of the high tribute paid to the art by a foreigner of the royal family of Pontus, who was visiting the Emperor on business, and had been among the spectators of this same pantomime. So convincing were the artist's gestures, as to render the subject intelligible even to one who (being half a Greek) could not follow the vocal accompaniment. When he was about to return to his country, Nero, in taking leave of him, bade him choose what present he would have, assuring him that his request should not be refused. "Give me," said the Pontian, "your great pantomime; no gift could delight me more." "And of what use can he be to you in Pontus?" asked the Emperor. "I have foreign neighbours, who do not speak our language; and it is not easy to procure interpreters. Your pantomime could discharge that office perfectly, as often as required, by means of his gesticulations."

The pantomime is above all things an actor; that is his first aim, in the pursuit of which (as I have observed) he resembles the orator, and especially the composer of "declamations," whose success, as the pantomime knows, depends like his own upon verisimilitude, upon the adaptation of language to character; prince or tyrannicide, pauper or farmer, each must be shown with the peculiarities that belong to him. I must give you the comment of another foreigner on this subject.

Seeing five masks laid ready—that being the number of parts in the piece—and only one pantomime, he asked who were going to play the other parts. He was informed that the whole piece would be performed by a single actor. "Your humble servant, sir," cries our foreigner to the artist; "I observe that you have but one body; it had escaped me that you possessed several souls."

I now propose to sketch out the mental and physical qualifications necessary for a first-rate pantomime. Most of the former, indeed, I have already mentioned: he must have memory, sensitivity, shrewdness, rapidity of conception, tact, and judgment; further, he must be a critic of poetry and song, capable of discerning good music and rejecting bad. He must be perfectly proportioned: neither immoderately tall nor dwarfishly short; not too fleshy (a most unpromising quality in one of his profession) nor cadaverously thin.

Another essential for the pantomime is ease of movement. His frame must be at once supple and well-knit, to meet the opposite requirements of agility and firmness . . . . The fact is, the pantomime must be completely armed at every point. His work must be one harmonious whole, perfect in balance and proportion, self-consistent, proof against the most minute criticism; there must be no flaws, everything must be of the best; brilliant conception, profound learning, above all human sympathy. When every one of the spectators identifies himself with the scene enacted, when each sees in the pantomime as in a mirror the reflection of his own conduct and feelings, then, and not till then, is his success complete. But let him reach that point, and the enthusiasm of the spectators becomes uncontrollable, every man pouring out his whole soul in admiration of the portraiture that reveals him to himself . . . .

Pylades and Bathyllus

John Weaver

> *John Weaver, 1673-1760, was an English dancing master and composer of pantomimes.*

PYLADES, BORN IN Cilicia, (as we learn from Suidas) was a very famous Pantomime at Rome, under the Emperor Augustus. He perfected, by some new Inventions, this Art of Dancing a whole play; for before Augustus's Time, the Pantomimes performed their Dances and Gestures while the Tragedy or Comedy was representing; but this Pylades, and a Contemporary [*sic*] of his named Bathyllus, were the first that left off all Actors, and introduced Dancing only on the Orchestra; and if we believe St. Jerome, Pylades was the first who danced at Rome, whilst others played upon the Flute, and while the Chorus sung;* and that before him the Pantomimes sung and danced themselves at the same time. He also wrote a Book concerning the Italic Dance which he had invented, and formed out of the Comic, Tragic, and Satyric Dancing. One may judge of his Skill in this Performance, when he consider that Augustus having recall'd him to Rome, (from whence he had been expelled by a Faction) did so please the People, that it was one of the Reasons for which they ceased to be angry with some inconvenient Laws which that Emperor had made.

Pylades had two Competitors, Bathyllus aforementioned, and Hylas who had been a Disciple to Pylades; and between them we find several Particulars concerning their Rivalship in Macrobius; and that there was a popular Insurrection upon account of their Jealousy; and that Hylas dancing one Day a Song that ended thus, great Agamemnon: expressed the Thing by the Posture of a Man who should measure a Person of great Stature. Pylades, to find fault with him, cry'd out, You make him a tall Man, and not a great Man; and was forced by the Audience to dance the same Song. He did it; and when he came to great Agamemnon; he assumed the Posture of a meditating Man.

Bathyllus of Alexandria, a Freedman of Maecenas, who loved him much, was a Pantomime of great Reputation, and was contemporary with Pylades, and assisted him in the new Method of Dancing entire Pieces. Suidas says positively that Augustus was the Inventor of this sort of Dancing, and that Bathyllus and Pylades were the first who introduced it; which ought to be understood, that Augustus authorized and established the Invention of those two famous Performers.**

---

*See comments on origins, pp. 15-16. —ED.
**loc.cit.

This new Invention of Dancing was called Italic, and comprized the Comical, Tragical, and Satyric Parts: Not that it was a Mixture of them, but each of these Pantomimes preserved the Character of each Sort in their Performance. Bathyllus excelled in the Comic, and Pylades in the Tragic Part; tho' oftentimes they were both concerned in Tragic and Comic; for it appears that Pylades signalized himself by representing a Feast given by Bacchus to the Bacchantes and Satyrs. The Emulation that prevailed between these two Pantomimes, formed two Sects that continued a long time; each left Scholars, who endeavored to make their Schools famous, and to perpetuate their Masters Name: The Spectators of Bathyllus were called Bathylli; and those of Pylades were called Pyladae: Both of them represented the Characters of their Masters. The Dances of the Former were merry, and fitted to amorous Adventures, and comical Subjects; and those of the Latter were grave, and proper to excite the great and more noble Passions of Tragedy. The Former stirr'd Lust in such a Manner, and gave such violent Temptations to the Female Spectators, that it occasioned these following Verses of Juvenal.

> One sees a Dancing Master Cap'ring high,
> And Raves, and Pisses with pure Extasy:
> Another does with all his Motions move,
> And gapes, and grins, as in the Seat of Love:
> A Third is charm'd with the new Opera Notes,
> Admires the Song, but on the Singer Doats:
> The Country Lady in the Box appears,
> Softly she warbles over all she hears;
> And sucks in Passion both at Eyes and Ears.
>
> The Dancer joyning with the tuneful Throng,
> Adds decent Motion to the sprightly Song.
> This Step denotes the careful Lover, this
> The hardy Warrior, or the drunken Swiss.
> His pliant Limbs in various Figures move
> And different Gestures different Passions prove.
> Strange Art! that flows in silent Eloquence;
> That to the pleas'd Spectator can dispence
> Words without Sound, and with Speaking, Sense.

A Roman Premiere
Charles Hacks

Charles Hacks was a physician, writer, and amateur player in pantomimes in France around 1888. The following excerpt from his book Le Geste, *is historical fiction.*

INTO THE SQUARE at the entrance of the Appian Way, before the Theatre of Mimes, the hurrying crowd rolled, broke, split apart like swirling, eddying waters. What a prodigious sight! From the height dominating the countryside one could see interminable lines of people, resembling miles of ants entering an ant hill, making their way to the theatre. Carriages of all manner and form ploughed the roads. The coming, going, crossing and swarming culminated in a black mass, sprinkled with grey dust and more antlike than ever, before the gigantic stone monument which, through its numerous colonnaded doors leading to its nine stories, was about to engulf more than eighty thousand easily accommodated, seated, souls.

All at once, without waiting for the theatre to be filled or the spectators to find seats, as though pressed to arrive at the main event for which the great crowd had come, the spectacle began.

There was first a sort of overture by the orchestra. The musicians, half-hidden under a thrust of the raised platform and without a conductor, embroidered their harmonies around each other's improvising. Rattles, tympani and flutes dominated, answering the calls of bugles and alternating them with silences in which echoed the notes of lyres. Then the chorus appeared; one by one they mounted the stairs to the stage for their song. They first arranged themselves in three rows of five, then five rows of three; they then made some diverse maneuvers, all the while singing various airs, joyous or sad, according to the indication given them by the guide or *coryphaeus*. The principal movement was very mysterious and consisted of imitating the revolutions of the heavenly bodies.

Then came the dancers, nude under a simple white veil of transparent linen. But no one paid them particular attention, neither to their bodies nor to their firm, round thighs, whitened by rubbing them lightly with chalk dust.

Suddenly the entire audience rose, for from the outside a wild acclamation was heard and stamping feet shook the ground. The mimes had just arrived, among them the celebrated Bathyllus, rival of Pylades and the other darling adored by the crowd. Decidedly the program promised to be exciting; because of the presence of his rival, Pylades

19

would certainly surpass himself. A magnificent ovation from one hundred sixty thousand hands thundered forth so strongly and was so prolonged that the sound of trumpets announcing the arrival of Augustus was lost in the din. The Emperor entered his box with his close friends, his poets Vergil and Horace, and his historians Quintus Curtius and Tibullus, but with no one paying any attention to him. Caesar in turn stood up to mingle his august applause with that of the populace in homage to the actor; the Emperor deferred to the comic, the mountebank, the mime.

Now All Rome was present, the Rome of theatre premières, the Rome of the Augustan era, The Mistress of the World; All Rome, her immortal poets, her wonderful historians, her conquering veterans of a hundred battles, all of them had come to watch a mime.

The small purple curtain between the *post scenium* and the stage opened slightly. A man emerged, rendered minute by the distance; he strode forward crossing the stage and the *proscenium*, more than 100 meters in length, and climbed onto the raised platform upon the stage where the principal actions of a play took place and where above all the mimes were positioned so that nothing of their art should be lost to view.

This actor was charged with announcing the play and, if it were a pantomime, outlining the plot. At his back, suspended by a leather strap, swung an enormous, hollow-sounding object—the mask which he donned as soon as he faced the public. Shouting through its bronze mouthpiece, he turned first to the Emperor: "Hail Caesar!"; and then to the people: "Hail to all! By the order, and at the expense, of noble Caesar, today the first day of Sextili, now named the month of August, a pantomime composed by Livius Andronicus entitled ROMULUS, will be played by Pylades the divine, and his troupe. You will soon be able to applaud them all, and give thanks to noble Caesar.

"As to the play, here is the catalog." And the actor, who up to now had recited his patter in slow and measured tones, suddenly raised his voice and poured glibly forth in a nasal falsetto.

"Primo: Proca, king of the Alba Longa, had two sons, Numitor and Amulius. Numitor being the elder, Proca left him his realm; but Amulius drove away his brother and seized the throne. To deprive him of a successor he forced the daughter Rhea Silvia to consecrate herself to Vesta; nevertheless she was delivered of twins, Remus and Romulus.

"Amulius, being informed of the event, quickly imprisoned the mother and exposed the infants, committing them to the river Tiber. However, at that moment the waters had just overflowed and were beginning to ebb, thus depositing the babes on the sands of the shore. The country offered naught but vast wilderness. A she-wolf appeared in response to the wailing of the two sons of Rhea; it pleased her to lick them and to offer them her udders, thus fulfilling toward them the duties of a true mother.

"This wolf, returning ceaselessly to the infants as though to her own young, was remarked by Faustulus, shepherd to the king. He followed her and found the children; thus they were brought to his thatched hut and raised by his wife, Acca Larentia.

"Secundo: The pantomime is divided into two tableaux and was written by Titus-Livius Andronicus.

"Tertio: Pylades will play the role of Faustulus; Dyonisia that of Acca Larentia. The wolf comes from the land of the Gauls and belongs to the actor Zoster, freedman of Procus.

"Quarto: Pylades will appear only in the second tableau and will mime the Hymn to the Child, newly composed by himself. I have spoken."

All this was heard in deep silence; they fairly drank in the words without missing a syllable. A pantomime with Pylades—ah, that was quite something!

Then the cheerfulness of the mob emerged for a moment, like a safety valve opening briefly, relieving in advance the concentration and sustained attention to follow. Retaining the actor on stage they baited, according to custom, that unfortunate stage handyman. "Bow! Bow!" shouted the crowd from all corners, and the unhappy man far down on the platform bowed very low in all directions. "Bow to Caesar!" And he quickly went about it. "Salute the Vestals! The Senators! The Knights! The magistrates, the people!" came the successive commands, and he accordingly bent this way and that, until suddenly a voice pierced the tumult, crying, "Look, actor, salute this!" All eyes flew up in the direction of the words, to the ledge of a cornice, and there fixed upon an astonishing, uncommon sight. Potbellied Varus, the unimaginably fat Varus who sold salt pork in the Velabrum under the porticos, well known to all Rome, had just turned around in his place and raised his toga to reveal, resting on the stone balustrade, his two huge buttocks, tumescent, inflamed, and reddened from his having been so long seated.

Homeric laughter rocked the house at the obscene and vulgar sight; the women emitted shrill little cries; everywhere, from top to bottom, the rows of shining bald heads and big paunches were jolted convulsively as rhythmic waves of laughter shook the theatre. The Emperor, with no thought for his majestic person, laughed loudest of all.

The actor took advantage of the debacle to make his escape. Then a whole mass of people filed onto the stage from the rear and up the stairs from the orchestra. There came men dressed as warriors, their bodies covered with animal skins, their feet bare, each wearing a leather helmet fastened by a glittering belt. Before them marched a mime of the second order (without shoes), who played such general utility roles. He was not masked. He looked very small, and having daubed his face with lampblack to simulate a fearsome chieftain, he lost what little physiognomy the enormous distance from the public had left him. Gesticulating with his arms he showed his men, explaining that he commanded these awesome and invincible fighters. And continually, in order to indicate their force and power, he used the same obscene gesture: the simulation of a phallus or rather a priapus in erection was executed with the left hand placed on the right upper arm over the biceps at the humero-cubital juncture, while the lower arm, fist closed to represent the phallus, was successively raised and lowered.

Performers wearing shoes trimmed with iron stamped to the rhythm of a march as shepherds, fishermen and hunters armed with iron spears flowed onto the stage. Finally the court itself appeared, preceded by masked clowns whose grotesque contortions frantically besought the laughter of the public. Amulius was followed by his brother and his niece in Vestal attire, and two slaves carried the two infants in a large basket.

There ensued a rather confused scene in the course of which Amulius drove away Numitor, caused Rhea Silvia to be loaded with irons and sent to prison, and ordered the wailing twins to be exposed upon the waters of the Tiber. The long, diffuse spectacle with its perpetual dull tapping of shoes, the rain of shrill sounds of fifes embellished with the drone of the pedal-organs seemed to lull the people. They peeped not a word; eyes wide open, they contemplated all that deployment (at a given moment there were more than two thousand people on stage), gently moving their heads in time to the music in a sort of rapturous trance of sight and sound.

Again the sets were pivoted to show now a clump of rocks overhung with century-old trees, and a murmur ran through the theatre. Eyes were directed upstage as, launched from a large boulder which served as a bridge, a she-wolf bounded upon the stage. There was an *ahhh!* of gratification from the spectators; the first really interesting mime had just appeared. The music stopped. The wolf hesitated a moment, searching among the actors feigning astonishment at her appearance. She saw the two slaves leaving with the basket which still contained the infants; in a rush the animal overtook them and savagely bit one slave on the thigh. He screamed and fell, covered with blood, and the wolf made for the second slave who ran and dodged, dragging the basket with him. At the same time the warriors and hunters attempted to impede her, but the wolf twisted and turned, jumping over and around them, eluding and doubling back, leaping like the wild beast she was, without once losing sight of her prey. She played her role to perfection and a thunder of applause was her reward. She succeeded in escaping the surveillance of a cordon of hunters and finally decamped at full speed in the direction of the fleeing slave, and followed by all.

The audience warmed to the sight of spilled blood; calls of approval and encouragement revealed their obvious pleasure in the cruel suffering. The bleeding slave was gathered up, wounded leg dangling, while slobbering Varus, glowing with emotion and pleasure, bawled from on high: "Death to the slave! For the wolf all my salt pork!"

The second tableau began with the precipitous arrival of the wolf. She was panting, unkempt, with bloodshot eyes, like an animal escaping a long pursuit. For some seconds she rove the stage, snorting and sniffing as though scenting a trail. When she stopped, hind-quarters to the public, ears down, staring fixedly at the rear, a slave appeared and called out the single word "Pylades."

But already the entire theatre was on its feet, and when the mime appeared an indescribable uproar and thunderous applause rent the air. From the imperial box overhanging the stage fell an avalanche of flowers, hurled by slaves who had brought them in great baskets. Huge handfuls were thrown by Vergil, Horace, Quintus Curtius, Tibullus, and the Emperor himself. "Pylades, you are divine!" cried Vergil. "Your memory is imperishable!" shouted Horace, as Caesar applauded. A group of courtesans, recognizable by their painted faces with the eyebrows joined by a black line of antimony, were wild with excitement. They held their breasts with both hands and troated loudly as they stamped their feet. Slaves gathered up the flowers as Pylades, object of this monstrous ovation, remained standing, the wolf crouched at his feet.

He was known to be admirably made, with a beardless, pale skin, shaven head, with the hair plucked from the sexual parts and underarms; effeminate yet strong. But none of this could be judged from the manner in which he was dressed. His head was completely hidden under an enormous, frightful, wooden mask having only one eye; its mouth was thrust forward to form a miraculous little trumpet, flattened at the end like a pig's snout. Nor could anything be seen of his body. It was covered with what appeared to be a leather diving suit finished to resemble natural skin and roundly padded underneath. Over this were animal skins representing a shepherd's costume, the whole looking like an outlandish goatskin bottle. Despite his inflated size the head still seemed disproportionately huge. His bare hands and feet were small and groomed like those of a woman, rubbed with cuttlebone powder, lime-whitened, the nails burnished with gold powder.

Such was the god, the idol of the hour—a fat stuffed doll suitable for frightening away sparrows.

Now a religious silence reigned. The audience gazed, nearly hypnotized, awaiting the moment that this ugly, potbellied deity should move. Twice he inclined his head, saluting first Caesar and then the public. A muffled murmur flitted briefly through the people, intent and scarcely breathing, and the interrupted program recommenced.

The wolf rose quickly and stood, ears pointed, tail wagging. Then Pylades began to mime. Standing with feet together and using only his hands and arms, his upper body swayed lightly with the movements as his head followed the gestures. He first presented himself, explaining who he was: a shepherd living alone on the deserted land where no one ever came, with only two companions, one devoted and sincere and the other a disagreeable, cruel, bad-tempered enemy— his wife, and the wolf. But it was his wife who was ferocious and the animal who was his friend. He mimed all of it simply, in one breath as it were; his gestures were slow, precise, and admirably articulated. The great head continually went from the audience to the wolf, in a motion at once sad and caressing. His arms seemed to be detached from the stuffed silhouette, that grotesque deformity which had been deliberately sought in order to enlarge the man proportionate to the colossal expanse of the stage. One was no longer shocked by his ugliness; it seemed to fade like a mirage, a *trompe-l'oeil*, so much did the man adapt himself to his gigantic milieu. So great a spell did he cast that the mask itself seemed at times to be animated.

As he mimed he was followed intently by the intelligent animal at his side. Exactly like an affectionate trained dog she cocked her ears and gently wagged her tail each time that the artist, with an indication of his finger, spoke of her. Pylades stepped back and his enlarged gestures said: "When she (designating the area from which his wife was to come) is not here we play, we two, like children. Look!" The wolf understood and jumped to attention, and there then took place between the man and the animal a short game of feint and dodge, of attack and counterattack, with beats, pauses, themes and offbeats.

Then Pylades pretended to stab the wolf and she instantly played dead. When Pylades began to flee she leaped up and overtook him, making for his throat as though she would strangle him with her teeth.

The drama of man and wolf was a rhythmic, strangely captivating, evolvement. At its close Pylades, overcome by the wolf, fell as though wounded, and with a final, savage thrust she pretended to throttle him. Then came a truly curious scene, mimed entirely by the wolf. She stopped suddenly, disconcerted, looking at the audience and then at the man stretched out under her; she sniffed him, was seized by a growing anxiety, and finally began to howl in despair. The cries attracted the wife Acca Larentia, but the jealous creature guarded the "cadaver" of her friend. At last she fled, chased by blows of a pike.

When the man arose the couple played a long scene during which their two personalities clearly emerged; he calm and peaceful, she twisting about him like a Fury. One felt that if it were she who had "killed" the man, she would not have howled in despair.

During the quarrel the wolf reappeared, seemingly perturbed, circling around them and trying to attract the man's attention. But he was too engrossed to notice. The animal left the stage but soon re-entered, dragging a basket in her jaws; the two infants were in it and she placed herself over their heads, thus offering them her teats to suck.

The figures on stage froze at this point, to represent the well-known tableau sculpted on all the Roman shields of the First Epoch: *a she-wolf suckles two babes while an astonished man and woman look on.*

The scene hurried on. The woman seized the pike and ran toward the children to kill them but the man intervened, and thus began the essential part of the pantomime and of the entire program—a mimed monologue by Pylades, Hymn to the Child.

The mime carefully placed himself in the precise center of the platform to dominate the entire stage. He started with the birth, miming successively the infant's various ages, interrupting himself to represent the nurse, the mother, the father, then returning to his role of the child. He traced his growth as he reached the stages of puberty, citizen, Knight, Senator, Consul, and finally Emperor. His meticulous gestures, varied rhythms, and delicate pauses were truly beautiful to see.

The audience scarcely breathed, but watched entranced, throats dry with concentration, emotion and admiration. The people knew and understood this art; they grasped the smallest details of gestures and pauses and gave themselves to it utterly; they rocked when the mime simulated a cradle and stirred when the infant was shown to be frail as a reed; they matured with him into the man, the citizen; and they were carried completely away when Pylades, in a vehement and impassioned peroration, ran to the basket, seized the two babes and with a grand and dramatic gesture presented them to the populace as though to place them under their aegis: "Here, take them, they come from you, they belong to you, and like you they will be kings!"

Illusion flowed into reality; for artist and public alike the theatre disappeared. There remained only the national legend, the story of Romulus and Remus, the birth of The City, Mistress of the World. Pride and patriotism titillated , the people passionately relived their fabled origins. As the mime, out of breath, near the end of his strength but with a supreme effort still held aloft the two infants, the entire audience again arose and eighty thousand throats acclaimed the artist, and thus acclaimed themselves and acclaimed Rome. Above them prevailed the blustering voice of Varus, crying, "Pylades, I adore you! Take all my salt pork and myself, too, if you like!"

Figure 2. An Italian mountebank of the 17th Century (after Du Jardin).

II. Mime Through the Seventeenth Century

(To the actor) You think it is so easy to be quiet when you have had your say. I tell you it is the hardest thing there is, and that as a rule to see you at such moments is enough to drive one mad.

—Luigi Riccoboni

It has been conjectured that the actors of the Mysteries of Religion were mummers, a word signifying one who makes and disguises himself to play the fool without speaking. They were dressed in an antic manner, dancing, mimicking, and showing postures.

—Colley Cibber

In Shakespeare's days, a clown was a peasant gifted with innocence.

—F. Billetdoux

THE SECULAR DRAMA of the Middle Ages had its roots in mime: songs, dances, farces, and marionette plays were performed in market places, in fairs, on streets, and in public squares. Diatribes and fulminations by the church testify more to the popularity of the "obscene players" than to the effectiveness of the church ban.

The sacred drama of the Middle Ages also had roots in mime; in an age of general illiteracy and lack of knowledge of Latin, an effective teaching technique was to enact dramatically stories of scriptures and other religious subjects. Mystery, morality, and miracle plays, said to be "acted sermons," were done in the churches in the forms of *tableaux vivants* and pantomime because of their effectiveness, and were linked together with dialogue. By the twelfth century the performances moved out of the church into the churchyard, the squares, and the streets in order to accommodate the growing crowds that came to see the spectacles.

The spoken plays of the mummers, as they were called, allowed plenty of physical action, much as did the later *commedia dell'arte.* A typical mummers' play from Berkshire calls for a ritual combat between King George and the Turkish Knight (Bold Slasher). And when the Doctor is to draw a tooth, he does so "after much by-play."

Dumb show

A special feature of sixteenth century Elizabethan drama was the dumb show (pantomime) beginning with Norton and Sackville's *Gorboduc* in 1562. It was a highly flexible dramatic technique; sometimes it fulfilled a dramatic function by depicting such actions as murders, death, state ritual, dreams, or the supernatural. At times it consisted of a formal procession before a scene; or it summarized an entire scene before the latter was played, to emphasize the theme. Dumb show was used outside the written play structure or within it, or as a play-within-a-play; sometimes it put the play or parts of it into an allegorical version; it was also used to show off-stage actions. The fact that it could take on so many functions accounts for its wide use by Elizabethan dramatists. Probably the most famous of all is the "dumb shew" in *Hamlet.*

Commedia dell'arte

Then came the long-lasting popularity of *commedia dell'arte*, a spoken form of theatre with much physical action and pantomime, from about 1550 for over two hundred years. At first, beginning with

Angelo Beolco (1502–1542), known as "Il Ruzzante," it was usually an improvised version of the existing rustic farces, short plays on country scenes and with country characters. The servants Arlecchino and Brighella, the miser Pantalone, the Doctor, and the Captain evolved as stock types, along with several others. These character men wore half-masks; the young lovers and the female servant Colombina did not. Closely linked to ancient Roman pantomime, to carnival and to knockabout farce, *commedia* spread from Italy through western Europe, permeating the drama in other countries and bringing women back onto the stage.

In France, *commedia* came up against entrenched licensed theatres, which promptly called upon the authorities to prohibit the rival Italians from playing; the foreigners just as promptly devised ways to avoid the prohibitions. When it was forbidden to have more than one actor on stage, a second actor spoke lines from the wings; when spoken dialogue was prohibited, actors sang their text; when that was banned, they displayed placards with texts written on them. And so on. And always, throughout, were the mimed sequences and the *lazzi* (comic bits). Whatever could be done in gesture was done so, giving it a rich mix of meaningful action, body language, and acrobatic wit.

Commedia made its way to royal favor, and soon the French playwrights wrote down or translated everything in sight. Many of them composed in the popular vein; a number of Moliere's early one-acts are written plays based on traditional *commedia* plots and people. By the seventeenth century the rustic themes and characters had become more sophisticated, upper-class, and literary. France has had a long tradition of ambulant theatre extending to as recent a time as the beginning of the twentieth century; the plays are serious and comic, some of the latter being based on *commedia dell'arte.* A number of these plays were recorded between 1835 and 1914 and published in *Théâtre de Tradition Populaire*, Marseille, 1942.

In England, traces of *commedia* appear in some of Shakespeare's plots: in *Comedy of Errors, Twelfth Night*, and *Taming of the Shrew.* The same is true of other playwrights, and English pageantry, masques, and revels contain many pantomimic elements. The traveling "fit-up" troupes of the English countryside, still performing in the 1900s, employ the semimprovised Italian play form.

The Spanish too were fond of rustic farce and *commedia* companies. Lope de Rueda (?1510–1565), player and playwright, founded the Spanish form with his written *pasos*, using characters and stories "purely Italian and Renaissance." The Italian *commedia* company of Alberto Ganassa went to Spain and remained there from 1572 to 1577.

And still *commedia* traveled—Russia, Poland, Germany, Austria—wherever it could touch a chord of popular response to its joyous, folk-wise fun, through the seventeenth and into the eighteenth century.

Commedia players

Italian companies fanning out to Europe included the Gelosi, Uniti, Fideli, Confidenti, Accessi, and private troupes of some of the nobility. Its players emerge from the anonymity of the Middle Ages: among the best-known were Ganassa, G. D. Biancolelli, Tristano Martinelli, and Evaristo Gherardi as Arlecchino; Antonio Riccoboni as Pantalone; Silvio Fiorilli as Pulcinella; Francesco Andreini and Tiberio Fiolilli as the Captain; Isabella Andreini, Virginia Ramponi, Flaminio Scala (who recorded fifty of his company's scenarios), G. B. Andreini and Luigi Riccoboni as the lovers. Perhaps the most remarkable was Isabella Andreini (1562–1604), not only the greatest woman player of her time, but one of the most famous of all *commedia* players. With her husband Francesco she headed the Gelosi company, winning accolades for her talent, beauty, intelligence, and virtue; she wrote verse and plays, was an honored member of the Paduan Academy, and was feted throughout France and Italy by audiences, artists, poets, and royalty.

Commedia's mime or pantomime sequences were probably comic interplay, comic entrances and exits, farcical encounters, acrobatic shenanigans, and good-natured mayhem, very much like what we have seen in our own vaudeville, music hall, and circus.

Two Miracle Plays
Anonymous

THE IMAGE OF St. Nicholas is in its shrine in the church. A rich heathen approaches, deposits his treasure and calls on the Saint to guard it for him while he goes away on a journey.

As soon as the heathen has gone, robbers enter, stealthily creep up to the shrine, and silently carry off the treasure.

Soon the heathen returns; on finding his property has been stolen, he flies into a rage and upbraids and beats the image of the Saint which had failed to protect his treasure. But upon this the image moves, descends from its niche, goes out and stands before the robbers. Terrified by the miracle, the thieves return trembling to the church, bringing back all they had taken.

The Saint's image returns to its niche. The heathen is transported with joy; he sings and adores the image. A priest appears and bids the heathen worship God alone. The heathen proclaims his conversion to the true faith.

*   *   *

A cradle is placed on the altar, and beside it an image of the Virgin Mary. There are shepherds, carrying crooks and having with them real sheep and dogs. Some of the shepherds feign to sleep, some to watch their flocks, when suddenly all are aroused as a sweet-voiced choir boy, dressed as an angel, mounts the pulpit and from there, after a blast from the trumpeters, announces the birth of Jesus. Thereupon a number of singing boys posted in the galleries in the clerestory, and representing the multitude of the heavenly host, begin to sing "Glory to God in the Highest and on Earth Peace, Goodwill Toward Men."

The shepherds proceed up the church to the manger, where the midwives show the child Jesus and bid them proclaim His birth to the people. The shepherds adore the child and His mother, and then march through the church singing a hymn of praise.

Figure 3. A Commedia dell'arte scene.

Pantomime in Italian Comedy

Paul Hippeau

Italian comedy, or Commedia dell'arte, *was a semi-improvised theatre form containing much physical action.*

TRUE THEATRICAL PANTOMIME did not actually reappear in France until the sixteenth century, around 1576, with the first troupe of Italian actors sent by Henry III to Blois, no doubt to distract from politics the members of three orders during the regime of the States.

Pantomime had a certain place in Italian comedy. The play of facial features, postures, gestures, were, for many, the reason for the favor enjoyed by the players, and the *lazzi* formed a large part of the plays in their repertoire. Many centuries before, in the time of King Theodoric, it was already a question of "those histrions who gave so many slaps, and blows with sticks, who reeled off their words, and invoked more laughter by grotesque movements of their bodies than by the more or less fortunate sallies of their wit." The various personages of the Italian comedy descended in a straight line from those histrions. Often their jumps, turns, and somersaults took the place of cues; the cudgelling was not spared and most of the famous actors of the *commedia dell' arte* were top-notch gymnasts. The *Gelosi* brought in by Henry III provided in many respects the Roman tradition.

In Rome, the pantomime actors wore masks of their own size, and appropriate to their roles. These masks did not have the open mouth like those of the tragic or comic authors; for that reason they called them *masques muets*. Some characters of the Italian comedy also wore masks. The paintings from Pompeii show the pantomimes lightly clad, in various poses, utilizing much muscular force and exhibiting beautiful plasticity.

But while they conserved the recollections, costumes, and attributes of the ancient grotesques, they invented new caricatures, new satiric parodies. Beginning with the platform stages, the come-ons of the Fairs, masquerades, and carnival amusements, *commedia dell'arte* modernized and perpetuated that group of popular, now cosmopolitan, types. Bologna, the University city, gave birth to the doctor, the ridiculous pedant; from commercial Venice came Signor Pantalone, the old merchant, pompous or miserly, but always duped; Spain, then occupying a part of Italy, furnished the Moor-killer, the *Miles Gloriosus* of Plautus; Naples gave the tricky, impudent, scheming servant, the *Zanni* containing the tradition of the ancient Theatre. Other towns, like Bergamo, furnished the best types of comic stupidity. We find again those characters, fundamental to the pantomime: they are called Cassandre, Gilles, Pierrot, Arlequin, Colombine, Trivelin, etc.*

We conclude, then, with the learned Charles Magnin, whose teachings are of great import, that "the popular, plebian drama in the squares, under the open sky, never failed to brighten up the sad lives of the serfs and the short leisures of the villagers; indestructible theatre that lived again in our day and in the open air galleries of Deburau; theatre that unites the ancient and modern stages. In the *joculatores*, *delusores*, the *goliardi* of our day and the Middle Ages, scholarship can find the most honorable ancestors in Greek, Latin, Oscan, Etruscan, Sicilian, and Asiatic antiquity, from Aesop, the Phrygian hunchback sage, to Macus, the jovial and deformed Calabrian, heroes of Atellan farce, since then become, on the streets of Naples, by the simple translation of his name, the very spightly Seigneur Polichinelle."

Dominique and Scaramouche were the two most celebrated mimes of the *commedia dell'arte* . . . . However, the Italian comedians did not play the pantomime as Deburau later did. The *commedia dell'arte* entailed spoken plays, or rather scenarios of plays on which the actors improvised. The *lazzi*, sprinkled throughout the dialogue to amuse the public, were less witticisms as we know them than colorful, fanciful pantomime.

---

*French names for Pantalone, Pedrolino, Arlecchino, Colombina, etc.

The Italian Theatre

Evaristo Gherardi

Evaristo Gherardi (1663–1700) played the role of Arlecchino in France. He published a collection, Le Théâtre Italien, (1694): scenarios, texts, and lazzi, written in French and Italian. The following excerpt comes from the preface to the collection.

THE ITALIAN ACTORS LEARN nothing by heart, and for the acting of a play, it is enough for them to have seen the subject for a moment before going on the stage. In fact the greatest beauty of their pieces is inseparable from the action, the success of their plays depending entirely upon the actors, who embellish them more or less according as they themselves possess more or less wit, and according to the good or bad situation in which they find themselves when acting. It is this necessity of acting on the spur of the moment which makes it so difficult to replace a good Italian actor when unfortunately he fails you. There is no one who cannot learn by heart and recite upon the stage that which he has learned, but something very different is required in the Italian actor. To say a "good Italian actor" is as much as to say a man who has depth, who plays more from imagination than from memory, who composes, while acting, all that he says; who seconds and supports whoever is with him on the stage, that is to say, fits his words and actions so perfectly to those of his comrade that he instantly enters into all the acting and movements which the other requires of him in such a manner as to make everyone believe that they were prearranged.

It is by no means the same with an actor who plays merely from memory. He never comes upon the stage but to recite as quickly as possible that which he has learned by heart, and with which he is so much occupied that, without paying attention to the movements and gestures of his fellows, he always goes his own way, in a furious hurry to deliver himself of his role as if it were a burden which fatigues him too much. One may say that such actors are like scholars who come, trembling, to recite a lesson which they have carefully conned; or rather, they are like echoes, who would never speak if others had not spoken before them. They are actors in name, but useless, and a burden to their company.

One must always draw a clear distinction between these actors in name and those real actors, who, though they indeed learn by heart, yet, after the example of excellent painters, know how to seek art with art, and who charm the spectators by their beauty of voice, truth of gesture, perfect flexibility of manner, and a certain gracious, easy and natural air with which they accompany all their movements and which they impart to all they utter.

Elizabethan Dumb Shows

Gorboduc, 1562
Thomas Norton and Thomas Sackville

> The order of the domme shew before the
> first act, and the significance thereof.

FIRST THE MUSICKE of Violenze began to play, during which came in upon the stage sixe wilde men clothed in leaves. Of whom the first bare in his necke a fagot of small stickes, which they all both severally and together assayed with all their strengthes to breake, but it could not be broken by them. At the length one of them plucked out one of the stickes and brake it: And the rest plucking out all the other stickes one after an other did easely breake them, the same being severed: which being conjoyned they had before attempted in vaine. After they had this done, they departed the stage, and the Musicke ceased. Hereby was signified, that a state knit in unitie doth continue strong against all force. But being divided, is easely destroyed. As befell upon Duke Gorboduc dividing his land to his two sonnes which he before held in Monarchie. And upon the discention of the brethren to whom it was divided.

Hamlet, 1601
William Shakespeare

> *Hoboyes play. The dumbe shew enters.*

ENTER A KING and Queene, very lovingly: the Queene embracing him, and he her. She kneeles, and makes shew of protestation unto him. He takes her up, and declines his head upon her neck. Layes him downe upon a Banke of Flowers. She, seeing him asleepe, leaves him. Anon comes in a Fellow, takes off his Crowne, kisses it, and poures poyson in the Kings eares, and exits.

The Queene returnes; finds the King dead, and makes passionate action. The Poysoner, with some two or three mutes comes in againe, seeming to lament with her. The dead body is carried away: The Poysoner wooes the Queene with Gifts; she seemes loath and unwilling awhile, but in the end, accepts his love. Exeunt.

Herod and Antipater, 1622
Gervase Markham and William Sampson

MUSIQUE: AND, Enter Egystus and Clitemnestra dancing a Curranto, which is broken off by the sound of Trumpets: then, enter Agamemnon, and divers Noblemen in Triumph: Egystus whispers with Clitemnestra, and delivers her a sleevelesse shirt; then slips aside. Clitemnestra imbraces Agamemnon, he dismisses his Traine; she offers him the shirt, he offers to put it on, and being intangled, Egystus and she kills him; then departs, leaving at Antipaters feete two Scrowles of paper.

Figure 4. Mei Lan-fang mounting an imaginary horse. (Courtesy Cecilia S.L. Zung.)

III. Mime in Asia

Mine eyes were dragomans for my tongue betied
  And told full clear the love I fain would hide;
When last we met and tears in torrents railed
  For tongue struck dumb my glances testified:
She signed with eye-glance while her lips were mute
  I signed with fingers and she kenned th'implied:
Our eyebrows did all duty 'twixt us twain:
  And we being speechless Love spake loud and plain.

> —The Second Kalandar's
> tale, Arabian Nights.

If one aims only at the beautiful, the flower is sure to
appear.

> —Seami

Acting is the art of standing still while not standing
still.

> —Ancient Chinese acting
> manual

40

IN ASIAN THEATRE, mime is so integral a part of stage forms that it is nearly impossible to talk of mime as such—it is simply a dramatic device used in all kinds of plays, from tragic to comic. Dance too is inseparable from drama; dance has acting-mime components, and actors are essentially dancers, or mimes, using defined, choreographed moves and attitudes, rigidly controlled bodies and rhythms, and with voice, stance, and gesture emanating from a single impulse.

China

Dance was the source of Chinese drama, beginning with social gatherings of tribesmen, or rituals before the altar. Ancient dances treated the subjects of harvest, war, and peace. Eventually professional dancers entertained the court and the gods, dances for the latter being performed in the temples and before popular audiences. Gestures, originally based on natural movement, became highly stylized; by the tenth century they resulted in a total theatre of poetry and prose, song and music, dance and pantomime. There were conventions for wiping of tears (with the left hand), for anger (pointed finger and stamp of foot), smiling (tracing the shape of a smile with two forefingers)— an entire language.

Japan

Japanese theatre was strongly influenced by the Chinese, but was not simply an imitation of it. It drew also on its own native sources, and on other Asian theatre. During the fourteenth century, symbolic religious pantomime, based on both secular and ritual dances, arose; blended with song and drama it became the elitist theatre of *Noh*, enjoyed by the court. The same period produced *Kyogen*, farcical dance-mime-sketches played as interludes between Noh scenes. Later, in the sixteenth century, came the *Bunraku*, or puppet, theatre, and the following century saw the emergence of *Kabuki* theatre—popular drama dealing with everyday themes of life and love, history, legend, and the supernatural.

Other Asian Countries

Mime is widespread throughout the rest of Asian theatre, as a few random examples will show. *Kathakali*, the mime-dance dramas of southern India, recall the heroes of classic mythical epic poems.

The *mudras* are codified attitudes and gestures of East Indian dance. In a devil dance from Ceylon (now Sri Lanka) the lead male dancer mimes the daily actions of a woman's life. Siamese dance divides gesture into three categories: those that express emotions, those of ordinary life, and those that indicate character intentions. Laotian dance contains four fundamental mime gestures: salutation, making up, flower taking, and walking. A Balinese flirting dance allows for improvised mimed sections.

Early in the twentieth century, European theatre practitioners "discovered" Asian theatre; among them were Paul Claudel, Jacques Copeau, Antonin Artaud, Jean-Louis Barrault, and Gordon Craig. The discovery had lasting effects—predominately an emphasis on physical aspects of theatre—upon each of these men, and upon later playwrights, teachers, and directors in France, England, and the rest of the theatre world.

Some Symbolic Actions
Cecilia Sieu-Ling Zung

Dr. Cecilia S.L. Zung was born into an upper-class Chinese home, and very early fell in love with theatre. Performer, writer, play-wright, teacher, and now a practicing lawyer, she was a delegate to the United Nations Commission on the Status of Women, 1947–1952. This excerpt is from her Secrets of the Chinese Drama.

CROSSING A THRESHOLD: The actor lifts his right foot high as if he were stepping over the sill. On putting his weight on the right foot, the left is lifted backward before stepping over. Then he has either entered or left the house. To play fainting, the actor should fall back into a chair, body very stiff. The sedan-chair: A big, embroidered curtain, held up on two poles by an actor, stands for a bridal chair or an ordinary sedan chair. The "rider" walks inside this curtain.

When men, usually of the official class, play riding in chairs, there are often four to eight servants standing on the sides of the stage. The leading servant first walks forward, stands facing the master, raises his right or left hand, and moves it sidewise in a big curve as if he were raising the curtain of the chair. At the same time the rider stoops a little forward and steps backward two or three feet, does the panto-mime of sitting down, before he advances, as if he were entering the chair and then riding forward in it. On reaching the destination, the servant goes through the same pantomime of pushing aside the cur-tain to let the rider out, while the latter again stoops, and then steps forward as if he were getting out of the chair.

To mount an imaginary horse: Raise the right hand "open" as if to stroke the "horse." Close the left hand as if to hold the "reins." Pass the third finger of the right hand into the loop of the whip handle. Then the hand clasps the handle. As the whip is drawn back, the left foot is lifted to the "stirrup." As the whip descends on the back, the right foot is thrown across the "saddle." As the rider is seated, the left hand tightens the "reins." The rider now faces the audience with an uplifted whip, ready to set out on the journey. To dismount an imaginary horse: Move the right arm and hand with whip up and toward the right in a big circle and then hold the whip horizontally in front with the left hand touching the tip of the whip. Simultane-ously, look at the audience as if saying, "I have reached my destina-tion." By a circular wrist movement turn the whip downward and to the right. When the circle is completed, slip the little finger out of the loop, and pass the whip to the left hand. Simultaneously, left the right foot as if the rider were dismounting. While the left hand does the pantomime of gathering the "reins" and receiving the whip, the left

foot steps as if getting out of the "stirrup." The whip is replaced in
the right hand "to be led away" by the rider's servant. Sometimes the
whip is thrown on the side of the stage meaning that the horse is let
loose to graze.

To show peeping through the window in the entrance gate of the
prison, the character, playing jailor, stands at the back of a chair, and
stoops to peep out through the space between the slats.

Admission into a prison: The jailor tilts the chair sidewise (meaning the prison door is opened) and then steps a little to the side so as
to let the prisoner (or his friend or relative) enter.

To get aboard a boat: The actor jumps forward and, while resting on
the floor, his body sways gracefully back and forth, in harmony with
the up and down movements in the knees, as if to balance himself on
the unsteady boat. Then he picks up the oar, placed on one side of the
stage. If two or more actors are in the boat, the leading one after getting
aboard holds out his oar horizontally towards the other, as if to provide him with a support. To anchor a boat: The actor, after gracefully
running in circles with an oar in his hand as if he were rowing, first
places the oar on the floor and jumps two or three steps forward as if
getting ashore. Then he turns about face, stoops down, and does the
pantomime of drawing the boat nearer to the shore and fastening the
rope to the pier.

To let down or roll up a curtain: The actor portrays the pantomime
of untying the fastening knots of the imaginary rope with which the
imaginary curtain is hung and of slowly unrolling the curtain by the
following movements: raise the hands high to the front, looking up-
ward; use the first three fingers of both hands to untie the imaginary
knots; then put palms up as if to hold the "rolled curtain"; gradually
lower the hands until the imaginary curtain hangs straight to the floor.
The actor stoops down to pick up the lower edge of the imaginary
curtain, rolls it up until it is high above his head and then fastens
it there.

Drowning in a well: A chair put on one side of the stage may stand
for a well. The actor mounts the chair, jumps down on the other side
and runs quickly off stage. Climbing over a wall or a hill: A table with
a chair at the side is put on the stage (never in centre) to represent a
hill or the wall of a building. The actor first throws one end of a rope
across the table (received and held by the property-man) and then as
if clinging to the rope he mounts the chair and table respectively.

The lantern: The ordinary kind is merely a wooden frame, the
lower part of which is wrapped in red silk and the upper larger part
in green. It is carried about to represent night.

[Banners bearing identifying names or titles, or a word of emphasis, are sometimes hoisted behind the appropriate character.[Banners with designs of waves and swimming fish represent water. Actors usually appear in fours, each holding a water banner, and constantly shaking it so as to make "waves." To represent suicide by drowning, the actor jumps towards them. Then they fold the flags around him and exit together.

Each character type has its own peculiar way of being acted, for instance, a "tan's" smile is not in the least like that of the other character types. A "ch'in" laughs robustly and loudly; a "lao-shen" laughs sturdily and in a dignified manner; a "ch'ou" enjoys much freedom which is denied other actors, while a "tan" must smile charmingly and with more tranquility. As to laughing and smiling, there are the following twenty kinds:

1. To laugh happily.
2. To laugh coldly.
3. To laugh conceitedly.
4. To laugh jealously.
5. To pretend to laugh.
6. To laugh surprisedly.
7. To laugh hysterically.
8. To laugh coquettishly.
9. To laugh coyly.
10. To laugh brokenheartedly.
11. To laugh scornfully.
12. To laugh insanely.
13. To laugh treacherously—often performed by actors playing successful wicked roles.
14. To laugh heartily—the performer usually laughs aloud three times to show exceeding joy.
15. To laugh reluctantly—being dissatisfied at heart, yet feeling impossible to do anything but laugh.
16. To laugh grievingly—full of grief, yet without any means of expressing the feeling.
17. To laugh violently—the actor usually laughs three times with upheld hands, either empty or with objects.
18. To laugh uneasily—to hide embarrassment.
19. To laugh affrightedly—though already out of danger, the person is still overwhelmed with the recollection of his past experience.
20. To laugh flatteringly—commonly performed by the "slightly white powdered face" [crafty] character.

On the Mimique of the Noh
Motokiyo Zeami

Motokiyo Zeami (1363–1443) was a Noh actor and theoretician.
He learned his craft from his father, a well-known actor, play-
wright, and teacher. Zeami performed the priceless work of setting
down the texts of Noh plays; he composed the music and created
the dance movements as well. The plays became classical texts
for the schools of training for actors, and his Secret Tradition of
Noh, *from which this excerpt is taken, includes treatises on theory*
and history.

ONE MUST ARRANGE one's thought in accordance with the literal text. When it is a question of "seeing," one looks; when it says "advance" or "draw back," one puts forward or draws back the hand. If it is something like "to hear," one cocks an ear, so that if one has employed the body to conform to every point in the text, the action comes about spontaneously. Of first importance is the use of the body; second is the use of the hands; and third, that of the foot. One must moderate the behavior of the body to the melody and tonality of the song. That is difficult to make clear in writing. When the opportunity presents itself, one must learn it by observation.

First make it heard, then make it seen. In all *mimique*, the procedure is the interpretation of a text by gesture. Now, it happens that the interpretation by gesture coincides with the text—better, that the behavior takes precedence over the word. Audition and vision are transposed. If one first catches the ear of the public, and one plays so as to lightly retard the behavior, at that precise instant, when the auditive impression substitutes for the visual, is born the feeling that the interpretation is perfect. Let us take, for example, the action of "crying"; if after having spoken the word "cry" you bring your sleeve before your face so that you are slightly later than the word, you end with an action. If even before the public has distinctly perceived the word "cry" you bring your sleeve before your face, the word is extended beyond the gesture and consequently you end upon a word. Under those conditions the action finishes first and you present an abnormal sight. Thus, because it is appropriate to stay upon an act, it is said: "First make it heard, then make it seen."

First identify well with one's character, then mime his acts. When I say "identify well with one's character," I mean by that the various kinds of the *mimique* of the Noh. If you play the role of an old man, it is a question of taking on the aspect of age: you will bend your back, your steps will be uncertain, you will extend or draw back your hand with cramped gestures. You will compose, to begin with, the outline of the character, then you will execute the dance, you will interpret the actions and the song in making them come from your appearance. If it concerns a female character, the waist rather shapely, you will extend and draw back the hand with measured gestures; each of the members will move with delicacy, all violence banished from your heart, you will execute the movements of the body with suppleness. So, you will interpret the characteristic comportment of the personage of your role, the dance, song, and even the walk, in making them emerge from your silhouette. If it is a question of an impetuous role, it is the violence at heart, in extending your body strongly, that you will enact. For all the other character types of the *mimique* you must first study the manner of identifying yourself with your personage. Then you can interpret his acts.

Notes on Indian Dramatic Technique
Ananda Coomaraswamy

Art critic Dr. Ananda Coomaraswamy (1877–1947) has written extensively on art, culture, aesthetics, and the gesture language of Indian dance. The complete article was first published in The Mask.

THE MOVEMENTS OF THE Indian actor are not accidentally swayed by his personal emotion; he is too perfectly trained for that. His body, if you will, is an automaton; while he is acting, there is nothing natural —that is to say accidental or inartistic—in his movements or changes of expression. The movement of a single finger, the elevation of an eyebrow, the direction of a glance—all these are determined in the books of technical instruction, or by a constant tradition handed on in pupillary succession. Moreover, nearly the same gestures are employed all over India to express the same ideas, and many, perhaps all of these, were already in use two thousand years ago.

And there is the closest connection between these gestures and those of the images and pictures of the gods and angels. Many of these gestures—called *mudra*—have hieratic significance; equally in a painting, an image, a puppet or a living dancer or danseuse, or in personal worship, they express the intentions of the soul in conventional language. For example, the commonest hieratic gestures have such significations as "I give all," or "hold nothing back"; "Do not fear"; "Contemplation"; "Calling the Earth to witness"; "Discourse"; others represent specific objects, as animals, parts of the body, stage properties, attributes; others are the signs of invoking and welcoming, placing on a seat, restraining and detaining—all these gestures are made by the fingers and palms.

By means of these gestures, and others perhaps less rigid, but all perfectly familiar to the spectator, and repeated without variation by the same dancer on different occasions, or by different dancers, it is possible to express the whole range of human emotion, and of action resulting from emotion, and likewise to describe the personal appearance of a god or hero, and all his deeds, in a language which is perfectly artificial and profoundly touching—a language with which the joy or sorrow, the youth or age, the male or female sex of the "shower" has nothing to do.

I have never seen, nor do I hope to see better acting than I saw once in Lucknow, when an old man, a poet and dancer and a teacher of many, many dancing girls, sang a Herd Girl's "Complaint to the mother of Krishna." This famous dancer . . . sat on the ground and sang his poem. Picking up a scarf he used it as a veil, and no one could have remembered that he was anything but a shy and graceful young girl, telling a story with every sort of dramatic gesture of the hands and eyes. She told how Krishna had stolen the butter and curds, what pranks he played, of his love-making and every sort of naughtiness. Every feature of the face, every movement of the body and hands was intentional, controlled, hieratic; not all his own devotion for Krishna spoiled his art to the least degree.

It is true that Binda Deen is a man of genius and a great personal character, and so the better able to identify himself with his art, not the art with himself. But such an action song as this did not belong to him, or depend on his genius for its being, even though he may have composed the particular words of it; it belonged to the race, and its old vision of a cowherd god. Nor would it, nor any Indian acting, have had much significance for an audience not already familiar with all its episodes and ideas and all the conventional gestures (dramatic symbols) expressing them. But it is remarkable that once given the key to these gestures, they no long appear conventional at all but "natural," in the sense of inevitable . . . . If this art of gesture has endured so long in India, it is partly because it has been so perfectly formulated, but also partly because it endures in stone and bronze as well as in living memories.

IV. Mime in the Eighteenth Century

*Are not gestures the offspring of feeling and the
faithful interpreters of every mood?*
                                        —Noverre

*Sacred to Shakespeare was this spot designed,
To pierce the heart, and humanise the mind,
But if an empty house, the actor's curse,
Shows us our Lears and Hamlets lose their force;
Unwilling, we must change the noble scene
And in our turn present you Harlequin.*

*When Lun appeared with matchless art and whim,
He gave the power of speech to every limb;
Tho' mask'd and mute, convey'd his quick intent,
And told in frolic gesture what he meant.*

                                    —David Garrick

THE DIFFICULTIES PREVIOUSLY created by the licensed Paris theatres for the Italian *commedia* companies were also directed against itinerant companies playing the fairs in the early 1700s, the Foire St. Laurent and Foire St. Germain, for the growing popularity of the wandering players offered significant competition to established theatre. To combat the constant prohibitions initiated by the privileged Comédie Française and the Opéra, the fairground theatres utilized many of the same subterfuges as did the *commedia* companies. Their pantomimes became a genuine theatrical genre with its own actors, characters, and composers; and the players delighted to mock the licensed house actors through parody of their characters, gestures, and tragic intonations.

Pantomime received a healthy impulse from that necessity to survive the successive restrictions. At first it had to be complemented, in order to be understood, by a variety of techniques: placards giving text, or couplets sung by actors in the audience, and other devices. Whatever the expedient, they eventually served to improve the pantomimic play so as to eliminate verbal or signal methods.

After the middle of the century, pantomime of the fairgrounds moved into another area. Jean Baptiste Nicolet, son of a marionettist, mounted a performance similar to those of the fairs at a theatre on the Boulevard du Temple in Paris: little comedies in the Italian taste, with acrobats and rope dancers in the interludes. Thus began the reign of Boulevard theatres and, in the early 1800s, the period of Jean-Gaspard Deburau.

Beginning of English pantomime

In England pantomimes were also called Italian Mimic Scenes, Night Scenes, or Night Pieces because they were brought to England by the same itinerant actors from the French fairs, usually during the off season on the continent. Also, when Italian companies were expelled from France in 1697 because of a fancied insult to Mme. Maintenon, they simply went to England and other European countries.

Actor John Rich (1692–1761), unsuccessful in playing straight drama, turned his attention to pantomime. He became famous under the name of Lun, and his pantomimes were said to be "coherent and witty." His serious pieces were called genteel dancing, graceful and regulated, with characters from nature or ancient fable whose gestures revealed their manners, passions, and characters. Grotesque pantomimes used characters outside of nature, such as *commedia's* Harlequin, Scaramouch, and Pierrot, playing distorted and ridiculous

Figure 5. Covent Garden Harlequinade, about 1770.

actions with grin and grimace. These were wholly silent enactments of Harlequin's escapades with Columbine and other characters from the *commedia dell'arte;* scenes of romance, chases, and magical transformations. English pantomime enjoyed great success in the coming years, with enthusiastic popular audiences and admiring attention from poets, critics, and writers.

The English dumb show of the last century was next seen in "modern entertainments," as they were called by John Weaver (1673–1760). They consisted of "dancing, action and motion only, performed in grotesque characters after the manner of the modern Italians, such as Harlequin, Scaramouch, Etc." Weaver claimed to have offered the first English production, *The Tavern Bilkers* at Drury Lane in 1702, although no record of it exists. Weaver was a dancing master and author of many treatises on dancing. His book, *A History of the Mimes and Pantomimes* (1728), is an historical account of performers of ancient Rome, together with a list of "modern entertainments" on the English stage from 1702 to 1726. His pantomime *The Loves of Mars and Venus*, 1716, was described as "a connected presentation of dances in characters, wherein the passions were so happily expressed, and the whole story so intelligently told, by a mute narration of gesture only, that even thinking spectators allowed it both a pleasing and a rational entertainment."

Mime in ballet

Mime now received important artistic attention in the ballet. Jean Georges Noverre (1727–1810) was a French dancer, choreographer, and ballet master; he traveled to and influenced dance in many foreign capitals: Potsdam, London, Stuttgart, Vienna, Milan, and finally Paris. He made drastic reforms in stage costume by eliminating wigs and stuffings. Rather than designing a mere dance divertissement he restored pantomime as a vivid means of expression, and he stressed the importance of good music and creditable plots. Noverre referred to his compositions as *ballets d'action*, or ballets that were danced-mimed stories in which "a step, a gesture, a movement and an attitude express what no words can say."

Rich's Miming

R. J. Broadbent

John Rich (1692–1761), as "Lun," was the first English Harlequin.

JOHN RICH WAS THE SON of Christopher Rich, formerly patentee of Drury Lane Theatre, and when he came into the patent, with his brother Christopher, of Drury Lane, and after having ineffectually tried his talent for acting in the part of the Earl of Essex, and other important characters, he applied himself to the study of Pantomimical representations at Lincoln's Inn Field's Theatre. To retrieve the credit of his theatre Rich created a species of dramatic composition unknown to this, and, I believe, to any other country, which he called Pantomime. It consisted of two parts, one serious, the other comic; by the help of gay scenes, fine habits, grand dances, appropriate music, and other decorations, he exhibited a story from "Ovid's Metamorphosis," or some other fabulous history. Between the pauses of the acts he interwove a comic fable, consisting chiefly of the courtship of Harlequin and Columbine, with a variety of surprising adventures and tricks, which were produced by the magic wand of Harlequin; such as the sudden transformation of palaces and temples to huts and cottages; of men and women into wheelbarrows and joint stools; of trees turned to houses; colonnades to beds of tulips; and mechanics' hops into serpents and ostriches.

It is a most remarkable fact that of the Pantomimes that Rich brought out, all of them could be written down as successes. In the exhibition of his Pantomimes, Mr. Rich always displayed the greatest taste. He had also acquired a considerable reputation as a performer of the motley hero under the name of "Lun Junr," as he was so designated on the bills at that time, and he was the first performer who rendered the character of Harlequin at all intelligible in this country. To others he taught the art of silent, but expressive, action, the interpreter of the mind. Feeling was pre-eminent in his Miming; and he used to render the scene of a separation with Columbine as graphic as it was affecting. Excellent were his "statue scenes" and his "catching the butterfly"; so also were his other dumb show performances.

Ballet Pantomime
Jean Georges Noverre

Jean Georges Noverre (1727–1810) was a dancer, choreographer, and ballet master who made far-reaching reforms in the ballet. This excerpt comes from his Letters on Dancing and Ballets.

MY LETTERS WERE BUT the first stone of the monument which I desired to erect to that form of expressive dancing which the Greeks called pantomime. It is well known to what degree the art of moving an audience by gesture was carried by the ancient mimes. It leaves to each spectator the task of imagining a dialogue which is ever true since it is always in accord with the emotions received. This reflection has led me to examine with scrupulous attention all that takes place both at the performance of a pantomime ballet and at that of a play (supposing them to be of equal merit in their respective spheres). It has always seemed to me that in pantomime the effect is more general, more uniform and, if I may say so, more in consonance with the total feelings aroused by the performance.

There are, undoubtedly a great many things which pantomime can only indicate, but in regard to the passions there is a degree of expression to which words cannot attain or rather there are passions for which no words exist. Then dancing allied with action triumphs.

Hardly a notion has been preserved of those pantomimes so celebrated in the age of Augustus. If these great composers, unable to transmit to posterity their fugitive pictures, had at least bequeathed us their ideas and the principles of their art; if they had set forth the laws of the style of which they were the creators; their names and writings would have traversed the immensity of the ages and they would not have sacrificed their labours and repose for a moment's glory. Those who have succeeded them would have had some principles to guide them, and the art of pantomime and gesture, formerly carried to a point which still astonishes the imagination, would not have perished.

Since the loss of that art, no one has sought to rediscover it, or, so to speak, to create it a second time. More venturesome than they, perhaps less gifted, I have dared to fathom the art of devising ballets with action; to reunite action with dancing; to accord it some expression and purpose. History, legend, painting, all the arts may unite to withdraw their sister art from the obscurity in which she is shrouded; and it astonishes one that *maitres de ballet* have disdained such powerful assistance. The *maitre de ballet*, for his part, must continually rehearse a mimed scene until the performers have arrived at that moment of expression innate in mankind, a precious moment which is revealed with both strength and truth when it is the outcome of feeling.

Make your *corps de ballet* dance, but, when it does so, let each member of it express an emotion or contribute to form a picture; let them mime while dancing so that the sentiments with which they are imbued may cause their appearance to be changed at every moment. If their gestures and features be constantly in harmony with their feelings, they will be expressive accordingly and give life to the representation. Never go to a rehearsal with a head stuffed with new figures and devoid of sense. Acquire all the knowledge you can of the matter you have in hand. Your imagination, filled with the picture you wish to represent, will provide you with the proper figures, steps and gestures. Then your compositions will glow with fire and strength, they cannot but be true to nature if you are full of your subject. Bring love as well as enthusiasm to your art. To be successful in theatrical representations, the heart must be touched, and soul moved and the imagination inflamed.

The court and the village, the elements, the seasons, everything contributes to furnish it with means to be varied and to please. A *maitre de ballet*, then, ought to explore everything, to examine all, since everything that exists in the universe can serve him as a model.

Consequently, a well-planned ballet can dispense with the aid of words. I have even remarked that they chill the action and weaken the interest. When dancers are animated by their feelings, they will assume a thousand different attitudes according to the varied symptoms of their passions; when, Proteus-like, their features and glances betray the conflicts in their breast, when their arms break through the limited movements prescribed by the laws of technique, to move with grace and judgment in every direction, they will express in their appropriate positions the successive stages of their passions.

Finally, when they bring thought and genius to their art, they will become distinguished. Words will become useless, everything will speak, each movement will be expressive, each attitude will depict a particular situation, each gesture will reveal a thought, each glance will convey a new sentiment; everything will be captivating, because all will be a true and faithful imitation of nature.

A Pantomime Audience

Jonathan Swift

*Jonathan Swift (1667–1745), dean of St. Patrick's Cathedral,
Dublin, was an English satirist.*

Observe, the audience is in pain,
While Clown is hid behind the screen;
But when they see his whitened face,
With what impatience they rejoice!
And then they value not two straws
How Solomon decided the cause.
Should Faustus, with his imp behind him,
Enter the stage, they never mind him.
If Clown, to stir their fancy, place
In at the door his mirthful face,
Then sudden draws it back again,
Oh! What a pleasure mixed with pain,
You every moment think an age,
Till he appears on the stage.
He gets a thousand thumps and kicks,
In every action thrusts his nose,
The reason why, no mortal knows.
While teasing all, by all he's teased;
How well are all the spectators pleased,
Who in the motion have no share,
But purely come to laugh and stare;
Provided Clown, for there's the jest,
Be soundly mauled, and plague the rest.

Glaskull, the Edinburgh Butcher
Anonymous

THIS GLASKULL WAS ONE-EYED; he also passed for a man well versed in expressing himself by means of signs. The Spanish ambassador, having heard speak of him, wished to see for himself, and visited the man.

He approached Glaskull and raised one finger. The butcher, at that gesture, raised two fingers. The ambassador then responded with three fingers. Glaskull put forth his fist. The Spaniard then drew from his pocket an orange and showed it to his fellow conversationalist. Glaskull in turn pulled out a piece of oatmeal bread.

Upon which the delighted ambassador departed, showing marks of the liveliest satisfaction.

"What did you understand?" he was asked. "That Glaskull is an admirable man," he cried. "I presented one finger, wishing to say that there is but one God. He reminded me that there is also God the Father, in revealing two fingers. By my three fingers I urged him not to forget the Holy Ghost. He then closed his fist to make me understand that the three in reality are one. Changing the theme, I showed him an orange as a symbol of Providence that gives to man all that is pleasant and useful. His reply of a piece of bread demonstrated to me that the truly essential, the necessary, was preferable to the showy."

"What did you understand?" Glaskull was asked. "Your man is ill-bred," replied the butcher. "He showed me a finger to tell me I've got only one eye. I gave him two to explain that my one was certainly worth the two holes in his face. He put up three fingers, some nonsense about our having no less than three eyes between us. Irritated, I showed him my fist, but him, just to ridicule me, pulled out an orange, something we don't raise in this country. So I took out a hunk of my Scottish oat cake and was going to throw it in his face, when he took off."

Figure 6. Drawing of Jean-Gaspard Deburau in a pantomime sketch. (Courtesy Institut International du théâtre.)

V. Mime in the Nineteenth Century: France

Charles Nodier had seen "Le Boeuf Enragé" nearly one hundred times. At the first performance, he awaited the appearance of the ox until the end, and not having seen it appear, he went out to ask the usher. "Madame," he said, "would you tell me why that pantomime that I have just seen is called "Le Boeuf Enragé?" "Monsieur," replied the usher, "because that is its title." "Ah!" said Nodier. And he left, satisfied with the explanation.

—Dumas père

I adore the pantomime. I would, if I were a millionaire, build a little theatre, or rather, a candy box in rose-colored marble; the interior would be decorated voluptuously, and every night there would play pantomimes à la Watteau, with delicious music of the ballet.

—Horace Bertin

Here lies a player who, without a word, said all.

—Epitaph written for himself by Deburau, but not used

Resuscitate the old pantomime, that's easy to say. There's absolutely no pantomime without Pierrot, and does one have a Pierrot at one's fingertips? One can easily find a Cassandre, a Leandre, even a Columbine, but a Pierrot! And without Pierrot, goodbye to the idea of pantomime.

—Francisque Sarcey

I N PARIS, THE BOULEVARD du Temple was known fondly as the Boulevard du Crime for the number of staged murders, incests, rapes, and poisonings performed on its boards. The Parisian center of theatre, it acted as a satirical reflection of the turbulent times, filled with revolutions and restorations. The newly lifted royal restrictions which had permitted only two theatre establishments to offer spoken plays, allowed it to turn into a perpetual fair, with acrobats, animals, barkers, musicians, and bizarre acts. The dramatic freedom that ensued, allowing all theatres to produce all types of performances, led to many innovations and every kind of attraction. Even pantomime had added to it dialogue and musical themes. However, in 1807 new restrictions were imposed and Napoleon allowed only a few theatres to operate as such, with their established separate repertoires. The minor houses again confined their offerings to nondramatic acrobats, clowns, musicians, animals, magicians, and pantomimes. Not only were silent pantomimes a legal necessity, but another law required that all performers in the nonfavored theatres, whatever the program or part, enter on stage with a somersault, or on the tight rope, or walking on their hands.

When the Théâtre des Funambules opened in 1816, a family of acrobats named Deburau, from Czechoslovakia, was hired. In 1819 the son, Jean-Gaspard, substituted by chance in a minor role of a Pierrot character. Gradually his development of Pierrot, whom he called Baptiste, pleased the crowds; it eventually formed a model of French pantomime, an idealization of which has come to us through the film *Les Enfants du Paradis (Children of Paradise)*, 1945.

Jean-Gaspard Deburau (1796–1846) created Baptiste as a slender, pale, elegant jack-of-all-trades involved in fantasy farcical situations; he seized the hearts and minds of the Boulevard patrons, from the street urchins to the literary elite. Even after pantomime as such suffered a decline in audience estimation, verses and music then being added to turn it into melodrama, his popularity at the Funambules continued and his audiences remained faithful to their Baptiste until his death.

During its peak years and after, a number of writers, poets, novelists and critics were enamored of the pantomime: Théophile Gautier, Théodore de Banville, George Sand, Champfleury, Charles Nodier, Jules Clairville, Emile Zola. Gautier (1811–1872) wrote *Shakespeare aux Funambules (L'Art Moderne*, 1856) and the sketch *Marchand d'Habits*, made familiar to viewers today in the above-mentioned film about Deburau.

After Deburau

Pantomimes were maintained at the Funambules with Paul Legrand and Gaspard's son Charles Deburau, but its waning popularity eventually sent Legrand on tours and the young Deburau to Marseille. There Charles, and his student Louis Rouffe, and *his* student Séverin, kept pantomime alive, albeit with words added and characterization changed. Séverin brought it back to Paris in 1890. Séverin (1863–1930) was a mime of tradition. He idolized Louis Rouffe, his teacher, all his life, and took the name by which the latter was known, l'Homme Blanc, for his own. He referred to traditional mime with its determined conventions as *mime d'école*. His most popular piece was the same [Mar]*Chand d'Habits* that Paul Legrand had played toward the end of Deburau's time without much success. Séverin's mime, so well received in his native Marseille, was outdated in Paris and *Chand d'Habits* took hold as an amusing period piece.

Pantomime, replaced by vaudeville in public esteem, still had its faithful few in Paris. Raoul de Najac (1856–1915), "wealthy amateur," was part of a movement, along with Paul Margueritte (1860–1918), called the *Cercle Funambulesque*, a gathering of players and playwrights who were fond of the pantomime. They attempted to revive both the art form and interest in it; the *Cercle* sponsored performances of some eight productions between 1888 and 1890. Mimes Najac, Margueritte, Felicia Mallet, Paul Legrand, Pepa Invernizzi, the Larcher brothers, and Jane May were among the performers, the women achieving popular recognition in the pantomime of the *Belle Epoque* in the following decade. The *Cercle* represented a final gesture toward traditional pantomime, which would continue in a somewhat changed form before disappearing almost entirely early in the following century.

Deburau-Pierrot
Théodore de Banville

Theodore de Banville (1823–1891) was a playwright, drama critic,
and poet. Called "apostle of the pantomime, a devotee of that
charming disappeared cult," he wrote two volumes of poems,
Odes funambulesques, 1857 and 1869. Excerpted from Mes
Souvenirs.

PIERROT, AS YOU KNOW, was the handsome, gracious, svelte, ironic
Jean-Gaspard Deburau. That incomparable actor had what he needed
to charm the populace, since he was of the populace by birth, poverty,
genius, childlike naivete; but also he responded to the need for elegance and splendor that exists in primitive souls, and never a duke or
prince knew as well as he how to kiss a hand, touch a woman. Even
when he bowed piously before the Fairy who recited her strophes,
victorious, taking flight with her ruby wings, he dared to vaguely hint
the gesture of taking some familiarities with her, and the Fairy didn't
resent it, nor the public, so much was he the spoiled darling of
everyone!

I said "hint"; he never emphasized anything; he indicated his intentions by a spiritual gesture, and quickly went on to something else.
"Without haste, without stop" was precisely the motto of his exquisite talent. He wandered through the universe with the detachment of
an artist and poet, but when necessary, he showed his friends the
street urchins in the galleries that nothing human was alien to him:
then he cooked a cabbage soup, fought a duel, mended old slippers to
sheer perfection. The tupenny Children of Paradise threw him oranges;
he gathered them up, pocketed them with childlike glee, happy to
play along. One minute later he was the disdainful prince, a magnificent Don Juan, playing with a refined simplicity that often made our
nervous, excitable actors reflect.

The sets were forever changing—beaches, forests, castles, crowded
streets—by means of a frame that one turned behind a curtain, the
sets sinking below or rising into the painted sky. Since the wings
were extremely narrow, sometimes one would see the two hands of
the stagehand himself. And do you think because of that that the illusion was destroyed or even lessened? No, quite the contrary. Think a
moment, and you will see it's right; for the more that human life is
affirmed in the theatre, the more the public sees human beings thinking, living, and behaving like himself, the more he'll believe in what

is happening on stage. Whereas with the dreadful perfection of material objects, there is born an indifference toward those bits of wood
and cloth in which human life is not mixed.

The sets would change and in the light Harlequin and Columbine
would pass, trembling with love amid turbulent, busy crowds—he,
Pierrot, dressed in snowy white and pale of face; he, the great Jean-
Gaspard Deburau, he would delicately pick his way through delicious-
ly comic, lyric, silent scenes like telling the beads of the innumerable
rhapsodies of his poem.

Once he was a doctor, and would distribute frantically his infernal
pills. But soon, amid a nondescript troupe of sick people, he noticed a
young Parisian gentleman: sad, pale, anemic, without the will to live
and disgusted even with sadness. "Goodness!" said Doctor Pierrot,
"there's something quite astonishing inside his head!" With a scalpel
he neatly opened the head, detaching the upper part like a lid; from
that open-mouthed head one would see a frightened mouse scamper
away, running madly over the uneven boards of the stage.

All the modern hatred of war, all the jokes about soldiers, barracks,
officers' clubs, were contained in the pantomime "Happy Soldiers,"
in which Pierrot found himself conscripted into the meshing gears of
military discipline; he would resist like an intoxicated butterfly flut-
tering around a candle flame. I see him yet, doing his fatigue duty in
his enormous sabots and his fatigues, drowned in the manure heap,
brutalized by the corporals; and then at drill, his rifle crushing the
foot of this one, poking the eye of that one, and always being bested
by his fatigue cap.

Oh what an admirable valet was this same Pierrot, how he quickly
expressed the effrontery of a vulgar Ruy Blas, passing without transition to flat servility! He coddled, spruced up, brushed, polished his
master Cassandre, carefully removed the smallest speck of dust from
his frock coat and hat, after which he helped him through the door
with a surprising kick! When the same Cassandre entered his house
and gave him his hat, Pierrot took the head-covering with respect,
caressed it with his sleeve, smoothed it, blew the dust from it, then
overcautiously hung it on the wall, but on a nonexistent hook, which
permitted the unlucky tricorne to roll deplorably in the dust. For the
duty of the valet is to hang the master's hat in the proper place, but
not at all to ascertain if a hook is there. What more could Balzac say
to express the solicitous indifference of domestic service?

At other times were played pantomimes of adventures: of brigands,
fairies, genies, gendarmes, a mixture of legends, traditions, fables,
myths, and gods. In heroic mimodramas Pierrot was a country fellow,

timid and brave by turns, who, aided by an Amazon, cut the throats of all the sabre-wielding brigands, and in time to the musical rhythm.

During the next to the last tableau one could hear murmur, moan, and splash, and one sensed the freshness of water. And the street urchins, knowing what was being prepared, shivered with impatience. Finally the back curtain was raised, and there appeared an edifice three stories high, made of shells, rocks, and sculpted columns; from it tumbled cascades of crystal sheets of water, splendidly lighted, full of glittering spray. When the god of love, torch in hand, would marry Harlequin and Columbine before an altar painted in brassy gold, on which burned rose-colored flares, the enthusiasm of the spectators made it supremely magnificent. I have never seen anything better than this apotheosis of snowy or glowing transparent waters, already announced on the poster of the Funambules by that magic phrase: "The program will terminate in a waterfall spectacle!"

How to Listen to a Pantomime

Horace Bertin

Horace Bertin (pseud. for Simon Bense) 1842–?: theatre critic in Marseille and writer of pantomimes. This piece appeared in Les Soirées Funambulesques.

THE SCENE TAKES PLACE on some Sunday evening at the Alcazar Theatre in Marseille, when the pantomime program of Charles Deburau will be played.

The theatre is bulging, filled with smoke and drunken dialogues; each artist is greeted turbulently with yells and whistles. Finally the director orders the pantomime, and the curtain rises on *Pierrot in Africa*, one of Deburau's triumphs. A deep, almost religious silence immediately falls.

When a vaudeville, a play, or an opera begins, one still hears for a time some whisperings and conversations in the audience, and sounds of opening and closing doors. But, on the contrary, every time the curtain rises on Pierrot, the public will not tolerate even the slightest cough and, as though by some mysterious order, immediately imposes upon itself a rigorous, absolute silence.

And why? Why here precisely, where hearing plays an insignificant part? It is with the eyes and the intelligence that the public takes in the pantomime and even the music which comments upon and embellishes it. The spectator's attention is all the more unflagging since he himself invents the dialogue; to paraphrase Jules Janin in his *Histoire du théâtre à quatre sous:* in that mingling of thoughts and things, midst waking dream in which the author, stagehand and musician cause ideas to swiftly pass before him, he is beguiled as much as in a deep sleep. The word is very apt. There is a magnetic rapture in the case of a spectator who listens to a pantomime; he is impervious to everything around him, and in that dreaming stillness his total being is caught up by the silent play unfolding before him.

We believe that on the day we hear the voices of Pierrot and Columbine the spell would be broken and the dream would take wing; one would not listen to a pantomime because the eye and the mind would no longer be compellingly attentive. The attentive eye and mind—indeed, all is there . . .

Souvenirs of a Mime
Raoul de Najac

Raoul de Najac (1856–1915) shifted the leading character from Pierrot to Harlequin. Music with mime was becoming increasingly important. Excerpted from Souvenirs d'un Mime.

DID MY MODEST WORK begin a new era in the relations between libretto and music? Without praising myself as an innovator, I think I have contributed a great deal in giving music the important place it has today in pantomime.

Naturally, by pantomime I don't mean circus acts, acrobatic exhibitions, expositions of exotic animals; nor that of the music hall, nor pretty girls insufficiently dressed; nor of little Parisian scenes, exhibitions of young ladies who devote to the dramatic art whatever time the occupation of courtesan does not require. Generally, the latter have partners who announce themselves in the newspapers: "the celebrated, elegant, voluptuous mime, acclaimed by the entire world"; I invent nothing. These things have nothing to do with what concerns us.

By pantomime I mean the short comedies and dramas wherein the use of the word is done away with. So that you can follow the plot more easily, the music emphasizes the situations. When Pierrot weeps, the orchestra becomes sad; as soon as Pierrot begins to laugh, it expresses gaiety.

At the time that Jean Baptiste Gaspard Deburau reigned in the little Funambules theatre, the orchestra contented itself with marking, by tremolos, the entrances and exists of the actors. Then they played well-known dance tunes uninterruptedly, changing them for each new scene; but the actors paid no attention. Developing their parts according to the inspiration of the moment, they gave free rein to their fantasy. With experienced mimes, the program could only gain from it. It would not be the same with those with whom we deal today: young actors or amateurs. It would be imprudent to give rope to these merely amateur players, so the music they are obliged to follow keeps them from racing off with themselves.

In *Le Retour d'Arlequin*, as in all the pantomimes I've created, the interpretation is not the strict slave of the orchestra. I can improvise, providing that at certain points the gesture coincides with the measure; expressed at the same moment in my miming and in the score. That necessity does not interfere; it helps the public to understand me, and the composer collaborates in making the piece comprehensible.

Eating brings on the appetite. I had given much importance to
music; the musicians gave it still more. They made the mimes bend
under the yoke of their notes, like a singer's voice, like a dancer's
legs. In some ways their works became little ballets. No need of talent
to execute them; an accurate ear and a little flexibility would
be enough.

A journalist asked the aging Paul Legrand about the role of music in
modern pantomimes. He replied, "I think that it should be altogether
different. Music now is too regulated, too precise; it hems in the actor
like a vice and deprives him of the best part of his abilities in that his
gesture is limited to the musical measure. No personal wit, no imagination is possible any more. They do very fine things, it's true, but
it's no longer my pantomime."

To be talented and work hard, that sums it up, whatever art form
one cultivates. As for a professor of pantomime, it seems superfluous.
If you are not talented he will do nothing for you; if you are talented
he can stifle your personality. We do not express our sentiments in
the same fashion, and the way that is our own will always be the most
sincere. So, the professor will endeavor to inculcate you with his way.
The conventional gestures—which you should use as little as possible,
for the audience does not understand them—are easily learned. For
example, you don't need several lessons to know that for marriage,
your right hand makes the gesture of placing a wedding ring on the
third finger of the left hand.

If your gestures are clear and your mime original, you will become
a great artist. In my opinion it was these two qualities that gave
Deburau—pupil of his own self—his fame.

The art of making and playing pantomimes is very like blowing
soap bubbles. You succeed a moment, then nothing remains. So you
will forgive me for having tried, in the preceding pages, to postpone
the oblivion into which myself and my pantomimes are condemned.
Gesture passes, the printed word stays . . . a little. Unfortunately, the
printed word cannot translate the gesture. In the most obscure corner
of the theatrical cemetery will I have a temporary plot? I'm afraid not.
When I go off to play pantomimes in the other world, that tour will
escape the attention of the public.

Pierrot Yesterday and Today

Paul Margueritte

*Paul Margueritte (1860–1918) was a novelist who often colla-
borated with his brother Victor; he also wrote pantomimes and
appeared in them occasionally. Excerpted from* Mimes et Pierrots.

PANTOMIME, IS IT? It's curious, nevertheless. But look, it's dead, fallen
into farce, circus clowning. And yet, to translate thought by gesture,
by changes of the face—if that isn't a unique, a primitive art, and in
fact the starting point of theatre . . . . Mix into that restlessness,
modernité, excitement—come now, isn't that worth the trouble of
being a mime, like one is a singer or actor? Yes, I searched, I asked
myself, who's the actor *par excellence*, the one who by his nature,
his characterization, by tradition, represents human traits the best?
It's Pierrot.

Pierrot, who came from the Romans, the Atellans—*mimus albus*;
Pierrot, a French fellow of subtle satire, of mischievous laughter, of
ingenuousness-become-perverse, yet remaining guileless; Pierrot
made famous at the Funambules by Deburau the father, by Deburau
the son, by Paul Legrand, then by Alexandre Guyon, Rouffe . . . . But
now, Pierrot, he's finished; the last mimes are old and pantomime is
dead. Ah! To revive and transform it too!

Look, the cheerful Pierrot has seen his day. Pierrot the lover, Pierrot
the servant, Pierrot the funnyman—I want no more of all that. Tradition? Yes, well, it's extinct. It won't be the old Pierrot any more. I
know; it'll be another, you'll see. As for me, I've conceived the tragic
Pierrot. Have you seen the *Pierrot* by Henri Rivière? It's very good,
but his Pierrot is devilish, a Satan; my Pierrot is tragic. Tragic because
he's afraid, he is terror, crime, anguish. In fact, how is it that the idea
didn't occur to anyone? How could anyone not be struck by the quizzi-
cal walk of Pierrot, slipping soundlessly inside his loose clothing,
which in immobility takes on the solidity of stone; and above all, the
disquieting quality in his head of a plaster statue? Willette, Huysmans,
see his clothing as black, but no, no, he needs the white garment.

The Last of the Pierrots
Séverin

Séverin (1863–1930) was one of the last of the traditional Pierrots. He brought mime back to Paris from Marseille in 1890, and was the only one to play successfully in Chand d'Habits. *This interview was made in 1923 by Barrett H. Clark.*

THE GREAT MASTER of us all [was Jean-Gaspard Deburau]. I am a pupil of Charles Deburau's pupil, Rouffe. When Charles toured the south he played for some time in Marseille and there Rouffe joined him. *I* studied under Rouffe but I feel close to the original line for when I was a youngster (that must have been in the late sixties or early seventies) I was taken to see Charles. I remember only a fascinating and mystical figure in white—naturally, I can't recall details. I have one of Charles's costumes. It's yellow now, alas! Pierrot's costume is a white sheet of paper on which the actor must write; the piano on which he must play. The white mask of paint which Pierrot always wears is actually a part of his costume. On that too must he write. It is vastly more difficult to express emotions under this mask than with the naked face, but does not art thrive on the difficulties which it must surmount? Through Pierrot's mask the expression must be rather exaggerated: we strive for general effects and must therefore avoid what is petty and unessential. You see? It is for us to respect Pierrot's pale face. The naked face would introduce a discord into the perfect symphony of white.

Tradition in my art is not everything, but without it, where are we? Whether I am a great artist or not, I am by tradition of the line of Deburau. I am sometimes urged to become modern, to discard some of the previous traditions of the old pantomime. But I maintain that to be modern is to be of all time. Even [Gaspard] Deburau, great innovator as he was, was one of a long line that goes back to the famous mimes of ancient Rome and Greece. Each new mime is, naturally, of his own day; he cannot help it. Gaspard summed up the spirit of his age and so did Charles [Deburau]. That is why they were supremely great. Pierrot has developed from a clown into a symbol of all mankind, suffering the misfortunes of all men, enjoying life, and taking no thought of the morrow. He is an idealist, a glutton, a hero and a coward, an anchorite and a sensualist. He is universal.

I don't like to hear people compare motion picture acting to pantomime. The motion picture bears the same relation to my art that photography does to painting. Indeed, true pantomime on the screen is rendered unnecessary by the childish expedient of announcing in letters a foot high the significance of each change of expression—or what is taken for such—on the face of the actor. But you have Charlie Chaplin. He is the greatest of them all—and a true mime. He could do Pierrot to perfection. You have of course noticed that a deep undercurrent of pathos underlies almost everything he does. That is genius. He is a great artist.

VI. Mime in the Nineteenth Century: England, Europe

Three things are required at Christmas time:
Plum pudding, beef and Pantomime.
Folks could resist the former two,
Without the latter none could do.

— Old Pantomime playbill

Shakespeare's and Nature's words lay hid in night,
Anon Grimaldi comes, and—"all is right!"

       *   *   *

"He was grim-all-day, made 'em chuckle at night!"

   *   *   *

Pantomime, the one art-form that has been invented
in England, an art-form specially adapted to English
genius, is in itself surely as attractive as any
art-form that the world has known; and it is amazing
that no Englishman of genius has ever laid a finger
on it.

— Max Beerbohm

Pantomime expresses the movement of the soul; it is
the language of all peoples, of all ages and times. It
depicts, better than words, extremes of joy and sorrow.
It is not enough for me to please the eye; I wish to
engage the heart.

— Viganó

Whereas the name of Deburau means Paris, pantomime, and Funambules, the name of Grimaldi, at about the same time, across the Channel, becomes synonymous with English "panto," affectionate term for the form of pantomime that developed in that country.

Joseph Grimaldi (1778–1837), son and grandson of pantomime players, devised a clown of such appeal, who achieved such fame, that clowns are still called Joey, after him. Grimaldi transformed nineteenth century pantomime; in his hands the role of servant to Pantaloon, not an important character, became Clown, the principal role in a happy mix of practical jokes, gluttony, cudgellings, thievery, satire, and magical transformations. Joey himself was an acrobat, juggler, swordsman, dancer, singer, and mime; he made his props, designed and painted his scenery, choreographed dances and sword fights; he was also a serious actor, with Shakespearean roles in his repertory. After his death his unpublished memoirs were edited by Charles Dickens.

English pantomime was enthusiastically patronized—so much so that the famous actor David Garrick also played in them, wryly commenting that Shakespeare could not pull in the crowds but pantomime could! A production began with an opening story, usually a fairy tale, then devoted two to three hours to the harlequinade, consisting of scenes of love, frustration, and wild chase with Harlequin, Columbine, and other characters from the *commedia dell'arte*, and with stock characters Clown and Policeman. The two parts were separated by a transformation scene, a dazzling magical change involving elaborate machinery: a ballroom with couches and chairs became a coach and horses, a dark cave changed into a beautiful garden. In time the opening story became more important, the harlequinade less so. By mid-Victorian times the story was the whole pantomime, with one token mime scene of harlequinade. That too disappeared by the twentieth century.

The English troupe of the Hanlon-Lees brothers specialized in pantomime of poetic delirium. The six brothers, born from 1836 to 1848, began performing early on and evolved a style of incredible, breathtaking gymnastics in pantomime sketches. In the course of playing their acrobatic comedies they would collide together, hurl themselves, mount each other, fall, dash, and crush—all with serenely innocent faces. They were wildly showered with adulation in Europe and America, and sparked some philosophical comment from writers. Emile Zola found their pantomimes delirious but also troubling, with

Figure 7. Grimaldi in *Harlequin and Asmodeus.* (From a color print in the Bertram W. Mills Collection. Courtesy Arno Press, Inc.)

sadness under the laughs, for their poetic fancy went far beyond simple display of skill and daring as they satirized human foibles and frailties. Banville saw in their "impossible" gymnastics analogy to the poet's soaring bounding rhythms, to the liberating of the god and the beast in us, and to the harmony and precision of the master poet.

"So little and frail a lantern could not long harbour so big a flame," wrote Max Beerbohm upon the death of Dan Leno (1861–1904). This famous pantomime player first appeared on stage with his parents at the age of three, then worked up a dance act with his brother. The music halls were home, school, and life to Leno, champion clog dancer, comic singer, and dramatic actor. He began in pantomimes at Drury Lane and embarked on a long series of triumphs, including a command performance, specializing in travesty roles. "Endearing" and "lovable," said the public and the critics, with his combination of wistfulness and fun, intelligence and creativity, whether in scenes of wild confusion or in confidential monologues. At the early age of 43 his mind gave way, and he died soon after.

Mime in the USA

Mime in the United States was first imported from England and especially from France. The language difference posed no problem in pantomime, and the English variety was too reflective of national life and locale to travel well. So French dancers, rope walkers, fairground performers and mimes toured the capitals of early America. Alexandre Placide produced ballet-pantomimes, and played the roles of Pierrot and Harlequin.

George Fox (1825–1877), American-born clown, was called the "Grimaldi of America." He modeled his early pantomimes on those of the English clown and also on the Ravel troupe, a popular French ballet-pantomime company. Fox was best known for his long-running production of *Humpty-Dumpty*. Other Americans appeared: Tony Denier played in pantomimes for twenty years, featured in harlequinade tricks while touring with P.T. Barnum. James S. Maffitt modeled his pantomime sketches on those of Pierrot and of Grimaldi, even to the costumes.

Mime in Europe

A curious vestige of nineteenth century pantomime exists to this day in the Tivoli Gardens, Copenhagen. Based originally on *commedia dell'arte*, it came to Denmark with certain modifications: Pantalone became a wealthy burger called Kassander from the seventeenth century French Cassandre; Harlequin and Columbine became the principal lovers in place of the traditional Isabella and Lelio; Pierrot became the central figure. The form dates from the English period of John Rich in the early 1700s. These *commedia* pantomimes were not unknown in Denmark at that time, but the definitive basis of Danish pantomime appeared there in 1800 with Giuseppe Casorti, who was then joined by Englishman James Price of the Price circus family. In 1843 the Tivoli Pantomime Theatre opened, and continues today under the guidance of dancer-choreographer-director Niels Bjorn Larsen.

Mime and Dance

In the tradition of Noverre was Italian-born Carlo Blasis (1797–1878), dancer, writer, choreographer, and theoretician who enjoyed a long, full career throughout Europe. Like Noverre, he emphasized the importance of pantomime in the ballet. Blasis was a prolific writer, publishing many volumes on dance technique, history and philosophy, literature, and biographies of theatrical personages, illustrating the textbooks himself.

Grimaldi
Anonymous

*Joseph Grimaldi (1778–1837) made the English pantomime
famous; he bestowed the generic term "Joey" on the character
of clown. This excerpt comes from* Popular Entertainments
Through the Ages.

HIS EYES, LARGE, globular and sparkling, rolled in a riot of joy. His
mouth, capacious, and as if endowed with a never-ending power of
extension, seemed fitted to express every physical enjoyment or dis-
gust. His nose! But who can portray that mobile proboscis? Its contortions, its twistings—now lateral, now upwards, now downwards,
now broadening, now contracting, as disdain, anger, fear or joy worked
in his grinning countenance. Grimaldi's nose! —we think we see him
now, screwing it on one side, his eyes nearly closed, though twink-
ling forth his rapture, and his tongue vibrating in his capacious mouth
in the very fullness of enjoyment. His chin, too, he had a power of
lowering, we will not say to what button of the waistcoat, but the
drop was an alarming one.

Grimaldi, besides being the clown of clowns, possessed qualities of
by-play, pantomime, or dumb-action, which placed him on a far higher
grade. It was in this respect that John Kemble used to declare him to
be the finest pantomimist and low comedian in the world. With the
single exception of the by-play of Edmund Kean, nothing comparable
to that of Grimaldi had ever been seen on the British stage. It was in
the art of subtle and graceful gesticulation that John Kemble [of the
Kemble actor-family dynasty] took private lessons from Grimaldi, as
did Lord Petersham and other noblemen and gentlemen of the Court.
I once saw Grimaldi, on a benefit night, give the dagger scene in
Macbeth. It was a darkened scene introduced in a pantomime, and he
was in his clown's dress. Notwithstanding which, and he only made
audibly a few elocutionary sounds of a few of the words, a dead silence pervaded the whole house, and I was not the only boy that trembled. . . . At another time he "commanded a regiment" with such an
air of hauteur, and in such unintelligible tones, that a private message was sent from the mess-room of the Horse Guards to the manager
of Covent Garden, threatening the withdrawal of patronage if Mr.
Grimaldi was permitted to continue "his d——d infernal foolery."
One more. During the first week of a new Christmas pantomime, he
sang in a trio entitled *An Oyster Crossed in Love.* He sat on the stage,

close down to the lamps, between a Cod's Head and a huge Oyster
(the bass, which opened and shut its valves with precision); and all
the children visible in the front rows of the boxes shed tears as they
gazed on Grimaldi's woeful countenance, his ridiculous yet excessive
sorrow making its way palpably through all the grotesque paint.

The Hanlon-Lees Go To America
Paul Hugounet

The English troupe of the Hanlon-Lees brothers was popular in
America and on the continent. Paul Hugounet (1859–?) was a
mime historian and producer of mime events; these comments are
taken from Mimes et Pierrots.

THERE ARE TWO VERY distinct aspects of English mime: on the one hand
the fixity of the *tableau vivant*, and on the other the screamingly
funny, dizzying somersaults, faster than the eye can follow. I cannot
close this summary of "epilepsy in pantomime" without citing those
exceptional mimes who revealed to us the English mime in its most
complete form. I speak of the Hanlon-Lees brothers, whose memoirs
were written by Richard Lesclide, whose gestures were illustrated by
Regamey, and whom all Paris applauded at the Varieties and the Folies
Bergeres. But the incredible pranks of the English pantomime did not
occupy them exclusively. Remarkable mimes, at the same time they
were peerless illusionists; their famous experience of the talking
headless *Sphynx* was due to their collaboration with Barnum.

[They went to "do" America.] The Yankee at first showed himself
to be recalcitrant, the police made difficulties over posters, the printer
was demanding. What did the Hanlon-Lees do?

They dispensed with posters, which were quickly covered anyway
by other ones. After several days of mysterious labors, the six brothers
launched themselves on the streets and avenues of the Union, wearing immense shoes, the soles of which printed on the sidewalk at each
step: "See the Hanlon-Lees Brothers!"

At Baltimore the publicity was even more spirited and unexpected.
Three brothers climbed the Washington monument and, leaning on
the narrow parapet, contemplated the panorama of the city spread
below. From the teeming street some idlers looked up. Suddenly
George put his leg over the parapet as if to throw himself over. Henry
held him by the leg, Robert got into the act, and there were the three
brothers cavorting in empty space while everyone stopped to gawk at
their dizzying somersaults, their strange acrobatics. When three or
four thousand Americans were assembled, Henry rained down a deluge
of false dollar bills on which was printed the eternal invitation "See
the Hanlon-Lees Brothers tonight!"

The funniest part of the story—on climbing down from the column,
they found at the base a policeman who wanted to arrest George for
attempted suicide!

Figure 8. Dan Leno in *The Railway Porter.* (Courtesy Arno Press, Inc.)

Dan Leno
Jacques Charles

Dan Leno enjoyed only a short life of immense popularity in English Panto. Jacques Charles directed the Theatre de l'Olympia, *Paris, in the early 1900s; these remarks are taken from his* Cent Ans de Music Hall.

I HAVE KEPT FOR THE LAST Dan Leno, who was in a way the predecessor of all those I have just talked of, since he was born in 1861 and was, in the opinion of Max Dearly, who knew him, the greatest comic in English pantomime.

Dan Leno was born into the profession. He had a horribly wretched childhood, and all his life retained the mark of it. He made his first appearance on stage at the age of three, as partner to his brother Jack, his elder by scarcely two or three years. The two youngsters would dance for hours in pubs, for scatter money. In turn, they were permitted to sleep on the floor of an attic.

In winter, when it was too cold, the two children would have face-making contests to make each other laugh. "Nothing warms you like laughing," Leno would say, and all his life he put that axiom into practice for, no sooner off stage, where he had just raised many laughs, he would tell funny stories to amuse his pals in the wings. He always began his tales with his famous "Believe it or not" which set off the laughs. On stage he never stood still; he had quicksilver in his veins.

For the first time, in 1878, the name of Dan Leno appeared at the bottom of a poster, for the Pullan Theatre Varieties of Bradford, where he would dance against anyone [competition in clog dancing], and always exhausted his opponents.

In 1880 he was proclaimed champion of that kind of competition, after having danced six nights at a stretch. He remained champion until 1883 and only lost his title by an unfair decision. He then began to dance and sing.

George Conquest saw his number and engaged him for two pantomimes. After the tour with Conquest, he opened in 1888 at the Drury Lane where he remained the star to the end of his life. There he created the leading roles from "Robin Hood" to "Forty Thieves," always spirited, burning the boards.

But, as Max Beerbohm wrote, "So little and frail a lantern could not long harbour so big a flame." And Dan Leno, worn out before his time by his miserable childhood, died at 43 years, giving a tragic meaning to his celebrated song "Never More."

The Pantomime Theatre of Tivoli Gardens

Ronald Smith Wilson

Company member Ronald Wilson, mime, dancer, teacher, and choreographer, plays each season with the Tivoli and teaches in England.

FEW OF THE SPECTATORS who gather on fine summer evenings before the fantastic Chinoiserie theatre at the entrance of Copenhagen's famous pleasure gardens realize that what they see is unique, one of the most extraordinary survivals in the history of the theatre.

And what would an audience of sixteenth century Italians make of the metamorphoses their favourites have undergone? "Il Magnifico Signor Pantalone," the lecherous Venetian, has become Kassander, a respectable if somewhat miserly eighteenth century merchant. Of the intriguing servants only Pierrot remains. Whilst Columbine and Harlequin have been promoted from "below stairs" to become the spoilt daughter of the house and her penniless lover.

It was in 1800 that pantomime settled in Denmark. In that year the Casorti family and their company, consisting of 22 dancers, acrobats and clowns, performed at Dyreshausbakken, a fairground which still exists on the outskirts of the town. Their success was so great that they were commanded to play at the Court Theatre. "Harlequin as Mechanical Statue" was in their first programme and it can still be seen in Tivoli. Giuseppe Casorti, the Pierrot, was evidently possessed of extraordinary acrobatic ability; he could walk a tight rope bearing a chair and table, sit down in the middle, and eat a hearty meal. When as a boy Hans Christian Andersen saw him he was so impressed that he danced a whole pantomime for his mother. Even later in life Andersen created many delightful papercuts peopled by capering Pierrots.

An Englishman, James Price, whose performances consisted of line dancers, equestrian acts, and "Genuine English Pantomimes," established a theatrical dynasty which continues in Copenhagen to this day. He joined forces with Giuseppe Casorti and contributed "Harlequin as Skeleton," probably still the finest piece in the repertoire. For although "Casorti" has become the generic term for the Tivoli repertoire, the families Price, Petoletti, Lewin and many more contributed to what is a combination of French, Italian, and English traditions.

An alien import can hardly flourish unless it finds a sympathetic response in the national temperament of its hosts. It was in the person of Niels Henrik Volkersen that a truly Danish Pierrot evolved. He brought to the role a simple, earthy humour full of peasant guile which he perfected from the opening of Tivoli in 1843 to his death fifty years later. Around this immensely popular figure a number of new panto-mimes were created, in particular "Pierrot Crazy for Love," and a group of popular folk comedies and satires of topical themes. But to all intents and purposes the form was set which has been maintained to this day. The public identifies with Pierrot, and around him the other characters revolve: Kassander, old and miserly; Columbine, his beautiful daughter; Harlequin with half mask but sans wart and whiskers; the pedantic Doctor, swashbuckling Captain and other suitors for Columbine's hand. In the repertory of fifteen pantomimes which are revived regularly, there is surprising variety. As the plot is basically the same, it is often individual scenes and *lazzi* comic bits that are memorable, and these could be interchanged from one piece to another.

To act these plays there is a specific vocabulary of gestures. There are signs to denote each of the leading characters, to denote objects such as ladders, candles, chairs, keys, and actions like hiding, sleep-ing, drinking, and speaking. On meeting each other Harlequin and Columbine mime: "I love and will marry you." This is represented by each gesturing to the other, then to themselves; both hands are then placed over the heart and the action completed by the right hand pointing to the ring finger of the left. The problem of interpretation becomes paramount, as in speaking a hackneyed speech in a classical play the question is how to rediscover the original meaning and then give it its true inflection. The difficulty in classical mime is to preserve the style without it hardening into truthless mannerism whilst still contributing something original in the way of interpretation.

Although there has been some modernization with the introduc-tion of counterweights to fly backcloths and electric lighting, the majority of the startling transformations are carried out manually as they were in the eighteenth century. Appropriate wings slide in and out on grooves. The Magician can ascend on trap doors, which can also spout smoke and flames. A tree can change into a camel and then into a Giant, or a rock becomes a boat. There is a Black Box into which Harlequin can disappear and reappear at will; and a wooden trunk in which Pierrot is hidden, only to be squashed by a huge boulder so that when removed he is as flat as a pancake.

When Niels Bjorn Larsen took over the direction in 1956, combin-ing it with his roles of solo dancer and one of the Ballet Masters of the Royal Danish Ballet, the Pantomime Theatre found a perfect leader, a mime of international calibre, pre-eminent in both classical and modern styles. His familiarity with the Bournonville ballets, with their extensive mime scenes, is another link in the extraordinary inheritance of Danish theatre.

On light summer nights, to this fantastic theatre flanked by flowering chestnuts, come people from all over the world; they gather here to laugh at these old comedies which have been lost in the lands where they were created.

On Pantomime
Carlo Blasis

Carlo Blasis was an Italian dancer, choreographer, teacher, and writer; he was Director of the Imperial Academy at Milan. He wrote numerous books, including Theory of Theatrical Dancing, *from which these comments are taken.*

STUDY TO MAKE YOURSELF understood by imitating the form of the objects you wish to represent; and when that is not possible, point out as clearly as you can their use, etc., so that your beholders may understand what you wish to express without ambiguity: let all your expressions be precise and distinct. I am aware that many persons would be ignorant of the meaning of these artificial gestures which are not founded on passion or nature; but in that case, to raise a desire to learn their signification, the Ballet master, and those who represent his compositions, should exhibit pieces both easy and accurate, in order that the public, appreciating their beauty, may apply themselves to the *grammar*, if we may so call it, of this new language.

This is in some measure reasonable enough and might be done with no great difficulty in Italy, where the people are naturally inclined to Pantomime and where the actors already make use of gestures of *convention*. In France some length of time, and a course of deep study, would be required to attain the same degree of perfection. The French Pantomimists have adopted only a small number of gestures, of which the greater part are destitute of correct expression. Thus circumscribed in their means their art cannot accomplish its due end, which is to represent to the eye a picturesque imitation of all things. It is natural to the Italian to gesticulate; it is not surprising therefore, if the actors of Italy are superior to those of other countries, or if Pantomime is there carried to so great a degree of perfection as to be capable of expressing perfectly all the passions, with every object sensible to the sight. They are, however, most materially assisted by the gestures acquired by art, which have greatly enlarged the sphere of their performances.

Pantomime being incapable of producing any very striking effect, except when employed in expressing strong emotions, and objects easy of perception, the Italians have selected the most celebrated deeds of both history and fiction, the more deeply to fix the attention of the spectators: these magnificent pictures are always represented in a vigorous manner and are sometimes sublime. This system excites great interest in the Ballet, and renders the Pantomime department

85

important, at the same time increasing and varying the pleasure of the public.

The Italian, endowed by nature with deep sensibility and a vivid imagination, is fond of powerful impressions, and prefers the stately and pathetic style to the comic or even the pleasing. He is willing to be amused by theatrical representations, but he would rather be affected and hence arises the interest taken by him in the performance of Ballets. It may be observed that the Ballet has been more essentially assisted by the art of painting in Italy than in France; nor has the art itself lost anything by it, but on the contrary gained infinitely.

In France, however, lately, several of my friends have distinguished themselves for their Pantomime and have attained the same perfection in expressing the passions as I have witnessed in Italy. This need not appear extraordinary, if it be considered that man is everywhere nearly the same. The only defect in these performers was a want of sufficient gesture to express perfectly every circumstance; but this was less their fault than that of their art. Notwithstanding this, their description of sentiment was true, their features spoke, and their attitudes were gracefully conceived. I noticed that the best of these pantomomic performers were from provincial theatres; they were more industrious, and their stock of pieces was greater than at the capital. In Paris about a dozen pieces form their round of representation; at Bordeaux, Marseilles, Lyons, etc., every Ballet that has succeeded is performed: at Paris, on the contrary, those only are performed that have been introduced by private interest and favour.

A Pantomime must be simple, clear and correct, if it be meant for a faithful interpretation of our sensations. All that cannot be understood at the moment of the action is mere imperfection, which it is the Ballet master's duty to regard as useless. Pantomime, like dancing, has its different kinds. Gesture, look, carriage, in short, all the physical expressions, are not exactly the same in every person: they vary with the age, character, condition of the actor, who ought, therefore, to pay the strictest attention to those kinds only of which he finds himself more peculiarly capable. Unless the actor possesses certain physical qualities and a natural disposition to Pantomime, he cannot expect to see his endeavours crowned with success. It is an incontrovertible fact, that without the gifts of nature, it is impossible for us to become perfect in any one art or science whatsoever; but at the same time, though endowed with every requisite, were we to neglect the sage precepts of art, we should equally fail of our end. Those lessons formed into laws and established by ages of experience, are essential, nay, almost indispensable, to the attainment of perfection.

The great Longinus says "that nature is mainly instrumental in conducting us to the grand and sublime; but unless art takes her by the hand, she is as one blindfolded, knowing not whither her steps are leading her."

A player ought to study the genius, character, manner and customs of the various nations, the natives of which he may have to represent. Let nature be his constant model. The varied features of his countenance must exhibit the different sensations of his soul, and his eyes, particularly, must add to the expression of all those feelings which his gesture is intended to convey. The gesture of the mime being ever in accord with his eye, should, as it were, speak.

Every action in Pantomime must be regulated according to the music, which ought also to participate in the expression of the passions. The effect resulting from this harmonious union creates the most pleasing emotions in the spectator. Let the mimic and dancer, however, beware not to force this action in order to prove that they really are in accord with the music; all must be blended together, and the art concealed as much as possible. The accompaniment must possess the true tone and colouring of the pantomimic action.

The Ballet master must avoid in his compositions all that is exaggerated, dull, vulgar or trivial, particularly in subjects of a serious nature.

VII. Mime in the Twentieth Century: to 1950

Le silence, cette grace universelle, combien d'entre nous savent en jouir!
> —Charles Chaplin

The poet, like the sculptor, deals more with the speech or gestures of men's bodies than with their actions.
> —Rilke

My theory is to take away the text from the actor and make him work only on actions.
> —Stanislavski

All great Drama moves in Silence—
Events of the greatest magnitude and significance pass in silence . . .
There were no words wasted in the creation of the Universe,
neither can words create so much as an ant.
All Nature is silent when it acts,
and speech cannot take the place of action.
> —Gordon Craig

Mime is the stem of the tree that has branched into drama and dance. Music and speech are produced by movements which have become audible.
> —Rudolf Laban

The dance is the child of music, Pantomime is the Child of Silence. But, though they come from opposite poles, the dancer and the mime are running to meet each other.
> —Barrault

TWENTIETH CENTURY MIME really started with the *Belle Epoque*—
that aptly named, divinely decadent decade of the Nineties (actually to 1914 and World War I), of exquisite and of execrable taste,
of spectacle and Victorianism, and of some of the wildest flourishing
in the arts that had ever occurred in so short a period. In theatre alone
there were Sarah Bernhardt, Eleanora Duse, Ellen Terry, Gordon
Craig, David Belasco, Maurice Maeterlinck, Oscar Wilde, George
Bernard Shaw, Anton Chekhov, Arthur Pinero, Edmond Rostand,
Gilbert and Sullivan, and more, along with writers and composers
in great numbers.

The *Belle Epoque* adored its belles: female actresses, female dancers,
female mimes. There paraded across the stages a long line of dancers
and actresses, a great many of whom also appeared in pantomimes.
But in pantomimes of a changed sort. The vestiges of Deburau could
occasionally be seen, but the modern pantomime of Georges Wague
(1875-1965) satisfied better the public taste for the exhibition of
women and a more natural style of play—that is, without the stylization of white makeup and traditional Pierrot costume. Wague first
performed conventional mime, but developed what he called *Pantomime Moderne*, in which appeared Otero, Colette, and many others.
The pieces were staged, silent playlets, often melodramatic, devoid of
mime conventions, and played with bold, broad gesture. Mimed plays
offered more women's roles than did traditional pantomime, so their
numbers increased. Georges Wague was also a teacher and director;
he played in silent films directed by Louis Feuillade, as a mime and an
actor. He appeared in the first stage play to be filmed, *L'Enfant Prodigue* (*The Prodigal Son*), a pantomime, in 1906. Wague was professor
of mime at the Conservatoire, the academy for the training of actors,
and also at the Opéra Comique and the Academy of Dance. His
important contribution to mime was the concept that gesture be
linked with thought, bringing mime choreography closer to acting
technique. Wague was consulted by Barrault on the Deburau role for
Les Enfants du Paradis.

Early cinema

Actors were needed for the popular novelty just coming into being,
the moving picture. For the most part they came from the stage, especially the music hall. These performers soon became aware that
film acting had to be different from stage acting—smaller movement,
less projection, a more naturalistic style of play—and theoretical principles began to develop. Wague saw films as a continuation of mime,
and mimes were at first sought after by film directors because of their

Figure 9. Charlie Chaplin in *City Lights.* (Courtesy Institut
International du théâtre.)

facility in physical expression. The early films, especially the comedies, depended more on action than on words, and mimes were particularly skilled in techniques of silent communication.

Matching the *Belle Epoque* in its surge of bouncing creativity and zany, try-anything antics was the Golden Age of Comedy, the period of silent films from the early 1900s to the coming of sound in 1928. Little known in the United States is the first one of them all, Max Linder (1883–1925). Born Gabriel Leuvielle in Bordeaux, France, he starred in an endless stream of comedy shorts, some 350 up to 1914, the year of Chaplin's first film. Linder carefully studied his own early films in order to discover new cinematic techniques. The comedians who followed—Chaplin, Keaton, Langdon, Lloyd, and others—were indebted to this vaudeville-star-turned-film-comic for the economy and simplicity required by the intimate camera over the broader techniques of the music hall stage. Linder made two visits to the United States, in 1917 and 1921, where his film efforts were not successful. Nevertheless, he had established the model for the early comedies, and Chaplin and others have paid him homage.

Mime in theatre

Next came an important occurrence that influenced European theatre generally and that produced, either directly or indirectly, the famous French four of mime: Decroux, Barrault, Marceau, and Lecoq. The event itself, the school and theatre productions of Jacques Copeau, resulted from certain antecedents: Gordon Craig's short-lived school for theatre in Florence just prior to World War I, with its impressionist, non-naturalist, physical style, and similar creations by Nicolai Evreinoff and Adolph Appia. French director Jacques Copeau visited Craig's school, was much impressed, and remembered his impressions when he opened his own school, the Vieux Colombier, in Paris in 1921. In directing and in design Copeau moved away from naturalism and toward impressionism; his training program included a variety of movement techniques; work in masks and its physical aspect, mime, which he considered to be only a tool for training the speaking actor. The school of the Vieux Colombier continued for only a few years, but it was a seminal force in theatre training; its explorations and implications are not yet exhausted nor even fully appreciated.

Etienne Decroux (b. 1898) came to the Vieux Colombier in 1923, and there became interested in the meaning, beauty, and drama of body work; he wanted to establish it apart from written text, and began to develop a style, which he called *mime corporel*, as a technique and philosophy of movement, separate and valid as an art form. He also developed *statuary mime*, evoking visions of Rodin's sculpture, with the same visualized fullness of structural form. Decroux's isolated, segmented movements also suggest cubist facets and planes.

Jean-Louis Barrault (b. 1910) joined Decroux in 1931 for two years. Together they attempted to find laws for this new form, to explore the endless possibilities in the body, and to establish principles, rules, and conventions. Barrault then continued on his own path of acting, directing, and writing. After his role of Deburau (Baptiste) in *Les Enfants du Paradis* he performed no more mime, but his theatre work is always infused with a physical approach and wherever possible contains mimed sequences like one of many in *Rabelais*, 1970, in which actors mimed the movements of being aboard ship.

Europe

Clown and mime have always shared a mutual interest in silence and comedy, resulting in crossovers that make it difficult sometimes to distinguish between the two: clowns perform mime, and mimes do clowning. Among the best-known of the European clowns was Grock (1880–1959). Born Adrien Wettach in Switzerland, he saw his first clown at age seven, and his future was ordained. He began by playing for school friends and at his father's inn, as musician, acrobat, trapeze artist, tightrope walker, and juggler. Other clowns in the first half of the twentieth century were England's Little Tich, Carl Bagessen from Denmark, the French team of Footit and Chocolat, and the near-immortal Fratellini family.

The explorations and research into movement analysis, dance, mime, and other innovative forms done by Rudolf Laban (1879–1958) were influential in the understanding of motion in all kinds of human activity, from industrial work movement to dance and acting. Laban traveled to all the Central European capitals, creating dances, pageantry, schools, and movement choirs (a form of group dance). He developed a movement recording system, Labanotation, which is in current use. Escaping Nazi Germany, he emigrated to Paris, then to England, where he exerted a great influence on dance and movement training.

USA

The Golden Age of Comedy referred to earlier applied above all to the silent film comics in America: Charles Chaplin (1889–1977), Buster Keaton (1895–1966), Harold Lloyd (1893–1971), Stan Laurel (1890–1965), and Oliver Hardy (1892–1957). As reigning stars they *were* the

Golden Age. Other comedians added to its fame: Fatty Arbuckle, Chester Conklin, Charlie Chase, Ben Turpin, Harry Langdon, W. C. Fields, Larry Semon, Al St. John. And women players: Mabel Normand, Louise Fazenda, and Marie Dressler.

One of the most prominent comedians in the popular media was the famous Bert Williams (1875–1922). He starred in vaudeville, music hall, musicals, and Ziegfield's Follies for thirty years, singing and dancing, playing comedy sketches and pantomimes. As a black artist he broke ground that helped other black performers to participate to a small extent in the white theatrical scene. One of his best-known pantomime sketches was that of a poker game; he dealt out the imaginary cards to his imaginary partners, reacted to their bets and to his own cards, to calls, bluffs, wins and losses.

Angna Enters (b. 1907) began in the mid-1920s to "invent" mime without even using its name. She was a dancer and painter, and felt a strong need to bring her portraits to life through movement; she called her studies "dance-images" or "dance-forms." She toured her mime programs throughout the United States each year from 1926 to 1955, and concertized frequently in Europe. Her ideas, expressed in several books and many articles, are fully as appropriate today as when they were formulated; she conceived that form and movement result from images and meanings, that mind and body interact upon each other, that it is less important to wonder at life than to show the wonder of life; and other concepts, not all necessarily original but together composing a body of sound, contemporary principles.

At the same time Charles Weidman (1903–1975), "dramatic dancer," came to mime from modern dance. A principal dancer with Denishawn, he later joined Doris Humphrey to create the Humphrey-Weidman dance theatre. His humor and whimsy found expression in "kinetic pantomime," his staging of James Thurber's tales; mime also informed his other, more heroic, dances on social themes.

Today Red (Richard) Skelton (b. 1913) is so well known as a television performer that his long career as a clown and mime, starting at age ten, in medicine shows, tent shows, circuses, burlesque, vaudeville, radio, nightclubs, and motion pictures is overlooked. He made his Broadway debut in 1937 and started in films the following year, and television in 1950.

*　　　　　*　　　　　*

To show the concurrence of some performers in the first half of the 1900s: During the *Belle Epoque* and pre-World War I, Wague and Colette played at approximately the same time as Linder, the early

American film comics, Grock, Laban, and Bert Williams. During the 1920s Laban, his students Mary Wigman and Kurt Jooss in Europe, and Angna Enters and Charles Weidman in the United States, introduced mime as a serious concert, sometimes experimental, art form. Enters gave her first concert in 1926, the year that Laurel and Hardy first played together. In the 1930s Decroux developed his mime, at about the same time that Skelton and Lifar were pursuing their careers.

When the film *Les Enfants du Paradis* appeared in 1944, with its educated guess at reconstructing Deburau's style, and was followed by Marcel Marceau's modern Pierrot in 1947, the two events gave impetus to the contemporary wave of interest and participation in mime, a wave which has not yet crested. The Pierrot style dominated the mime scene for several years, after which individual creations outside of the French *Pantomime Blanche* began to appear, first in Europe and then in the States. The process continues . . .

Figure 10. George Wague, Otero, and Christine Kerf in *Giska la Bohemienne*, 1907. (Courtesy Tristan Rémy and Editions Georges Girard.)

Resources of the Silent Art

Georges Wague

Georges Wague (1875–1965) led the important shift from traditional pantomime to modern mime with his emphasis on acting concepts. He was the only performer to have spanned Pierrot mime, music hall, film, teaching, and present-day styles. This article was first published in the Paris Excelsior.

I SEEM ALWAYS to repeat the same thing, but it is necessary: whatever the form, the period, the music of the work in which one plays, you must have the ideas well in mind. Without the thought, the gesture is useless. Gesture is only the continuation of the thought.

The minimum of gestures corresponds to the maximum of expression.

In my opinion, everything is there. It is up to the teacher to substantiate the gestures and develop their application.

The art that manifests itself in mutism, Pantomime, has evolved like all the others, especially during these last fifty years. Dramatic art has been transformed with Antoine, Dullin, Jouvet, Baty. Lyric art still stagnates, to the great despair of composers who themselves are walking with giant steps. During this period, long for those of us who live it but so short a moment in Time, I was witness to four evolutions in the art of Pantomime.

First, the decline of the formula applied by Gaspard Deburau and his successors Charles Deburau and Paul Legrand; then the decline of the Marseille school, succeeded in turn by Bernardi, Bighetti, Thalès, that ended with Séverin, creator of *"Chand d'Habits"* by Mendès and Bauval. To these first two transformations is added another more complete one with the *Cercle Funambulesque*, of which the most representative artist was Felicia Mallet; she was for me an invaluable guide and cherished initiator, whose work I continue.

Then, for the third time Pantomime was queen. It was successfully being played in several theatres at the same time. *"L'Enfant Prodigue,"* *"La Danseuse de Corde,"* *"Scaramouche,"* *"Histoire d'un Pierrot"* all at the same time made the fortunes of their directors. Next, more brilliantly staged, *"Giska la Bohemienne, "La Belle Mexicaine,"* *"Le Coeur de Floria"* that I created with Otero, Kerf, and Regina Badet. Finally, still another genre: *"La Chair,"* *"Nuit de Noel,"* *"L'Oiseau de Nuit,"* *"La Main,"* *"L'Homme aux Poupées,"* *"La Bête,"* *"La Lime."* Violent dramas, clear, fast action that was easily read, with few characters. That style was all the rage between 1906

Dans les « *Cantomimes* » de X. Privas

Le Père Pierrot de *l'Enfant Prodigue*
avec Emma Sandrini et Marietta Ricotti
(1906)

Dans *l'Age d'Or* avec Christine Kerf

Le Pierrot Noir
du « *Couronnement de la Muse* »,
de Gustave Charpentier, de 1908 à 1951

Figure 11. The Pierrots of Georges Wague. Left Top: In *Cantomimes* by X. Privas. Right Top: The father in *The Prodigal Son.* Lower Left: In *Age of Gold.* Lower Right: Black Pierrot. (Courtesy Tristan Rémy.)

and 1914. It made known, besides Otero, Charlotte Wiehe, Lucienne Willy, Christiane Mendelys, Paul Franck, Jacquine, and our dear and great Colette.

Soon a new evolution. It is rumored that Pantomime is on the decline. Not true; it is simply changing. It borrows powerful aids: natural settings with infinite changes; it enlarges beyond measure the countenances of the players, it localizes the significant details of an action, a gesture, an attitude. The Cinema, insofar as it is silent, is but the extension of Pantomime; there the mimetic has more of a place than does trivial gesticulation.

But the soundless began to speak. Again the mimetic gave over to the verb.

Finally, in the last evolution, another conception came about. With *"Les Dames de Bonne Humeur"* of Scarlatti by Diaghilev, *"L'Amour Sorcier"* of Manuel de Falla, *"Triana"* of Albeniz by the Spanish ballet of the "sorcerer" Argentina, then the rivalry of Derain, and closer still *"La Table Verte"* [*The Green Table*], the ballet of Kurt Jooss—here is reborn, evolved, and triumphant the art of expressing sentiments by movement, gesture, and attitude. The composed, choral mime of *"La Table Verte"* produces a striking effect. It is presented as Dance, but in reality the profound impression that emanates from it is rather due to Pantomime, which is well favored in that new form.

That the diverse forms of Pantomime one after the other become obsolete, is inevitable, fateful; but Mimetic will exist for always, for it is the first and most moving means of human expression. I was spurned because thirty years ago I was writing that Pantomime should be human, not conventional. However, my applied ideas have borne fruit. If I were to repeat now what I advanced then, which seemed revolutionary at the time, they would doubtless take me for an old dotard.

Pantomime dying? Get along with you! Open your eyes, look around. It still has place in the long chain of the Arts but, like the others, it feeds itself on all the sciences, takes advantage of all the discoveries and techniques, constantly changing its visage but retaining its eternal soul. Only—and for the better—those Pantomimes or Ballet-Pantomimes succeed that have incontestable artistic value, or methods of expression that remain human.

Music Halls
Colette

*Sidonie Gabrielle Colette (1873–1954) is known, of course,
throughout the world as a writer. Less known is the fact that she
performed as a mime in music halls while establishing herself as
an author. She also spent several years as a drama critic. Her
success as a mime resulted from personal magnetism and natural
acting ability. The following essay is excerpted from* Earthly
Paradise.

WAS I, IN THOSE DAYS, too susceptible to the convention of work, glittering display, empty-headedness, punctuality, and rigid probity which
reigns in the music hall? Did it inspire me to describe it over and over
again with a violent and superficial love and with all its accompaniment of commonplace poetry? Very possibly. The fact remains that
during six years of my past life I was still capable of finding relaxa-
tion among its monsters and its marvels.

Everything in it was by no means as gay and as innocent as I have
described it elsewhere. Today I want to speak of my debut in that
world, of a time when I had neither learned nor forgotten anything of
a theatrical milieu in which I had not the faintest chance of succeeding, that of the big spectacular revue. What an astonishing milieu it
was! My contribution to the program was entitled *Miaou-Ouah-Ouah.
Sketch.* On the strength of my first *Dialogues de Bêtes*, the authors
of the revue had commissioned me to bark and mew on the stage. The
rest of my act consisted mainly of performing a few dance steps in
bronze-colored tights.

We are having a rehearsal in costume at the Theatre X, a pantomime that the advance publicity predicts will be "sensational." Backstage there is the smell of plaster and ammonia, and in the depths of
the dim abyss that is the auditorium, disquieting larvae move about
hurriedly. Nothing is right. The scenery isn't finished, it's far too dark
and swallows up the light and does not give it back; the spotlights
are unfocused, they make haloes; and oh, that rustic window gar-
landed with russet grapevines which willingly opens but refuses
to shut.

W.,* the overworked mime, does his *Dame-aux-Camelias* act, holding his stomach to repress a hoarse cough; his cough is frightening,
it scares you to death, that dramatic working of the jaws. Upset, the

---

*George Wague.—ED.

99

Figure 12. Colette in a Cat Pantomime. (From *The Difficulty of Loving* by Margaret Crosland; published by Peter Owen, London.)

Young Lover has applied poppy-red make-up to his nose, while his ears remain pallid, which earns him a string of epithets gasped out by the mime, W., who calls him, among other things, a blockhead, a duffer, a crackpot. Nothing is right, nothing will ever be right!

"And Madame Loquette?" exclaims the nervous manager. "What's happened to her?" "Her costume isn't ready," gasps the mime, W., in a stage whisper. The manager bounds and barks downstage, his chin jutting over the orchestra pit. "What's that? What's that? Her costume isn't ready? A transformation costume, when we open to-night? Things like this are enough to drive a man insane!" A shrug of helplessness from W., perhaps a gesture meaning farewell to life, with that cough of his! Suddenly the dying man leaps like a ball-player and recovers his voice to yell: "In the name of God, don't touch that! It's my knife for the red currant juice!" With the hands of a hos-pital nurse he grabs his trick dagger, a special stage property which bleeds sirupy red drops.

"Well! Here at last is Madame Loquette!"

Everyone rushes forward with exclamations of relief, toward the star performer. "Let's have a look at this famous costume!" It is a disappointment. "Too plain!" grumbles the boss. "A bit dingy!" the big moneyman lets fall. The composer of the music, abandoning *Pelleas*, draws near and says thickly, "Funny thing, I didn't imagine it like that. If I'd had my way, it would have been green, with gold, and, ah, with thingamabobs dangling, some . . . whatyoucallums, those gadgets, you know!" But the mime, W., enchanted, declares that this rosy red marvelously shows off the dull brown and gray of his smuggler's tatters! Mme. Loquette, a vague look in her eyes, says nothing, having only one desire in the world, and that is for a ham sandwich or two . . . or three, with mustard . . .

Disquieting news of a possible strike of postal workers, which will perhaps be followed by a railway strike? The company is in a fever of excitement and gossip, with each one outdoing the other in the wildest predictions. The least pessimistic predict a forced stop, and that terror of actors on tour, a complete breakdown that would leave them stranded . . .

We draw up futile plans of resistance and subsistence: an improvised performance that will pay our board and room; I will dance, our romantic lead will juggle knives, the first comedian will lift weights, the ingenue will sing ultranaughty songs. "It's my speciality at parties," she says. The property man, ex-*prix du Conservatoire*, will play his Chopin polonnaise that won him the prize, and our young and serious stage manager, remembering that he was a lieutenant in a crack cavalry regiment the year before, will demonstrate some *haute-école* on the best hack from a nearby riding school.

Not for a month have I seen so much cordiality, so much solidarity in the troupe; it is a surprise, a revelation. Faces that were inscrutable light up, sparkle with the wish to serve, to employ forces and talents that are rusting and about which only yesterday there would almost have been cause to blush: "As for me, I can tell fortunes!" "For my part, I can walk on my hands, and I've had practice as a fire eater!" "Me, I was a 'promoter' at the Alcazar bar in Limoges." Tomorrow, if the postal strike is averted, all this will be forgotten, we will talk about something else, the hoity-toity girl with experience at the Alcazar will recover her artlessness, and the acrobat will reassume his stiff and formal "British look" in his greenish overcoat.

The Cinema According to Max Linder
Max Linder

Max Linder (1883–1925) was the first international comedy film star. His style was that of dapper elegance combined with zany horseplay. These excerpts are taken from Max Linder.

I HAD THE THEATRE in my bones and, convinced that the stage would complete my theatrical education better than any professor, I wanted to begin absolutely anywhere, no matter how. At the *Ambigu*, after many attempts, I was able to meet the stage manager. An actor, over six feet tall with a thundering bass voice, was obliged to leave; the stage manager, who until then could do nothing for me, offered me the part at a moment's notice. With joyous heart I accepted; I spent the night studying and learning the sixty lines of his part, and rehearsed the next day. The stage manager gave me some vague instructions: "You are there, on the level, you make some big movements, and in a voice that could dominate the waves, you direct the maneuvers because your ship is going to sink straight down." I was so happy that I forgot to eat. Heart full of hope, I went back to the dressing room to dress. Alas! I forgot only one thing that day, to try on the costume of the actor I was replacing. I plunged into his trousers and I disappeared in his coat. The sleeves and pants were so long that I couldn't see either hands or feet. The coat reached to my knees and the trouser waistband came to my armpits. When I went to show this to the stage manager he answered, "Leave me alone! Work it out yourself! You go on in ten minutes." Ten minutes! And the costumer was absent! A dresser took pity on my distress, and tried quickly to pin up some false hems. Time was pressing, set changes were made in a blackout, I was pushed on stage and onto the level that represented the footbridge, someone put a cap on my head that came down past my ears.

The lights came up and there I was, rigged up like a clown! Everyone on stage burst into uncontrollable laughter. I spluttered. I couldn't hear the prompter but from the audience I heard quite clearly Grisier, who meant to watch my debut, cry out, "He's ruining my play!" And the curtain came down.

That grotesque failure, however, did not discourage me. The stage manager of the *Ambigu*, who naturally would not hear my name mentioned, hired me all the same to play in a melodrama; but I must admit that in order not to be recognized I wore a false nose! Between times I practiced dance, and with some success was able to perform a number consisting of comic dances.

102

Figure 13. Max Linder in *Seven Years Bad Luck.* (Courtesy Norman K. Dorn.)

A charming young man, Louis Gasnier, then stage manager in America, came one day to the *Ambigu* and said to me: "Would you like to make some pictures?"

"What's that?"

"It's like theatre, except that you play before a camera. You come, you make some jokes, you'll get twenty francs. Dress well: top hat, gloves, pearl tie pin, polish. I don't know exactly what you'll do, but very likely you'll be a young man about town paying court to a girl."

The night following that conversation it froze, cold enough to crack stones. Next morning when we arrived at the studio at Vincennes, Louis Gasnier told me: "We've found a terrific idea. The lake in the woods at Vincennes is frozen. You'll play the beginnings of a skater."

"But, old chap, I don't know how to skate!"

"That'll be even funnier," he answered. They put skates on me. They shoved me onto the ice before I could change my clothes. I I couldn't tell you what I did. I tried to stand up, but my hat fell off. I wanted to pick it up, I lost my balance and fell on my hat. On four feet, walking on my knees, I left the ice and regained dry land. I said to Gasnier: "Anything you like, but no skating!" He answered: "It's finished, we filmed your fall. It'll be very funny."

In fact, the film came out and got lots of laughs—at my expense. I can say "at my expense" because I received only the fee of twenty francs, and I had over eighty francs worth of damage; in those days a top hat cost twenty-five francs, my jacket was torn, and I lost my cufflinks.

I shot several comedies with the directors that Pathé assigned to me. They were liked by the public but for me they weren't quite right, to the extent that I refused to play what they offered me. M. Pathé asked me why. I told him. So he said: "All right, do it your way." Then I was able to give free rein to my imagination. I was nineteen years old. Cinema was in its infancy, and everyone knows how children do things the simplest way. Tell a three hundred-page story to a youngster, he'd turn it into twelve feet of film! Just think: I shot one film a day, about one hundred meters long. I was the author, director, player and prop man.

On the metro on my way to the studio I would unwind the reel of ideas. I had only to grab the end of the thread and I had the whole film. Often I reached Vincennes, the end of Line No. 1, without noticing it, the metro employees would remind me to get off. At the studio I'd give my scenario, demonstrate and explain it. We'd rehearse once and then shoot. No more difficult than that. And since our spectators were the same age as us, they were delighted. Go ahead and try to shoot a film in one day today! You need a whole day for a prop man to find a prop as simple as a stationmaster's loud speaker!

During this time, like other Parisian artists, I alternated playing in various music halls. That's how I was engaged at the *Olympia* where, besides my usual work, I did a boxing number on roller skates; I can scarcely describe how dangerous that was. It happened one night that I slipped and fell. Result: two years of illness, two years I had to spend alone, sick, conviced that my career was ended. However, I got better and as soon as I could I went to the Pathé brothers. I was ready to make every concession. Timidly I asked: "Would you sometime need my services?" But very soon I signed the contract of my dreams: a million francs in three years for fifty films a year.

Each Art Has Its Own Territory
Etienne Decroux

Etienne Decroux (b. 1898) has been called the grammarian of mime by his most famous pupil, Marcel Marceau. These comments are excerpts from "The Pretensions of Pantomime" in In Search of Theatre *by Eric Bentley.*

"PURISM" IS THE CORRECT view of art in general. In the world outside, in the universe, things are not separated, they exist in a jumble, together. But man does not accept this situation. Man likes difference. Man as scientist admits that things are "together" in the world but in the laboratory he separates them. Man as artist refuses even to admit things are "together" in the world. He is Prometheus and protests against the nature of things. He lives by the pretence that things are separate in the world too. He lives by separation. The law of art is not addition but subtraction. To add is to make a mess, to restore the original "togetherness" or disorder of the world. What is rich in art? Not a mixture: a purity. A single thing—which penetrates deeply. A single thing which leads to all things.

The law of difference is a law of economy. Life is too economical to repeat itself. Even a machine never repeats itself, one part never duplicates the work of another.

Each art has its own territory. Pantomime and dance are opposites. Dance is abstract and based on music. Mime is concrete and based on life. Dance flows like a stream. Mime moves with the natural plunge and lunge of the muscles. Dance is ecstatic and vertical, Mime earthy and horizontal. The dancer works with the leap, the mime with the walk. The dancer deals in symmetric patterns, exact repetitions, regular rhythms, as music enjoins; the mime in asymmetry, variation, syncopation, the rhythmic patterns of speech and natural body movement. Dance comes from excess of energy. When a bear paces to and fro in his cage he is finding the symmetric patterns of the dance in the customary way. A dancer is a man taking a walk—because his energies are not used up by his work—whereas a mime is a man walking *somewhere*, to a destination. Thus Mime is the energy it takes to turn the waterwheel; dance is the gay, spectacular splash of the excess water, the water the wheel does not need.

Watch dancers on stage pretending to carry a grand piano. They rejoice in the hollowness of the pretense. They trip along. The piano has no weight. Now watch mimes going through the same act. They present precisely the weight of the piano by indicating the strain it occasions.

The dancer is like *l'homme du salon*. Things are done to him. Thus, he does not walk, he *is walked*; all the normal symptoms of the adventure which is walking are eliminated, what we see is an imposed pattern. The mime is *l'homme du sport*. When a sportsman walks, you see what walking is; just watch his legs, and the way his arms move in concert with them! Your ballet dancer, like your *homme du salon* in general, has been trained *not* to make these movements, your mime is trained to display, exploit, and accentuate them, that is, to give them style.

Realistic? No. Art should not be too present. Poetry is absence. That is why memory is a good poet. Memory is at a distance, subtracting, adding, assembling. Art is like a dream.

To render spiritual fact by physical means. It is the mind's dearest luxury to imagine a world without causality—to defy gravity, for instance. The law of life is shock, impact—thus unbroken fluidity of movement suggests the unreal, the spiritual . . .

Language consists of arbitrary noises and symbols, which have to be learned. What we could use on the stage is vocal mime, i.e., sounds like cries and sighs—only more highly developed—which are in themselves expressive.

Figure 14. Jean-Louis Barrault in *Les Enfants du Paradis.* (Courtesy Institut International du théâtre.)

Dramatic Art and the Mime

Jean-Louis Barrault

Jean-Louis Barrault (b. 1910): mime, actor, director, writer;
perhaps best known to American audiences from his role of
Deburau in Les Enfants du Paradis. *This article was first published*
in Opera, Ballet, Music Hall.

ON THE EXTREME LEFT of the art of the theater there resides *the pure technique of gesture*, also called the art of *the mime*. To the extreme right is the art of *the spoken word—pure declamation*.

The art of the mime is the very Art of Silence.

In the art of the mime, two elements can create plastic values: on the one hand the gesture which is still an indistinguishable part of action; and on the other, that self-containing gesture which is the simile of a chorus in a tragedy, a matter for poetry, indeed transmuted into pure poetry. The difference between the one and the other is as great as the difference between prose and verse.

In 1953 it so happened that a dramatic version of *As I Lay Dying* was performed for the first time and could well be understood as a manifesto clamouring for a revival of the art of the mime.

It was by a study of the body that I was to broach the question of acting technique. Dullin's teaching drew our attention to the expression of the body. An actor must, in truth, submit himself to a period of training from which he will emerge more pliable, more knowledgeable in matters relating to the art of the gesture, better equipped to select and construe and impose rhythms upon a code of gestures which will harmonize with the spoken word.

Exactly like the spoken language, that of gesture has its grammar and its rules. Gestures do not duplicate, but they complete, the spoken word. During rehearsals, a whole code of gestures must be minutely drafted. It amounts, so to speak, to a secret, subconscious underground obverse of the actual action. Thus a plastic form of expression exists alongside that of the spoken word and the one can just as well complete the other as it can deny it, or blend into it.

The art of the pantomime, as it was understood of old, is a deaf and dumb art—modern pantomime is the Art of Silence.

In old-fashioned pantomimes, gestures were added over and above action itself, as by a deaf mute. The modern mime has a yearning for the pure, and denies itself the language of the mute. It wants to embody action and nothing but action and if anything is added it will be a kind of lyrical song of gestures, springing from an overflowing soul.

109

What is new about the modern mime is that it can reach up to tragedy. It becomes a noble art and to that extent can be truly compared to oriental mime. But in fact there is nothing oriental about it, there is simply the fact that it has reached a degree of dignity which makes it worthy of the comparison. When the art of the mime is at its height, for sheer beauty it can be compared to the most magnificent verse, the noblest music, the most admirable painting, the most perfect sculpture. It is an art that is pure.

It may well be that, following Charlie Chaplin, yet another form of mute pantomime shall be revived on the stage—there remains nevertheless the true problem that confronts the modern mime which consists in lifting the art of the gesture into the realm of tragedy.

The Art of the Gesture—it is a pure and genuine sapling of the tree that is Dramatic Art.

The Mime and the Dancer

Serge Lifar

Serge Lifar (b. 1905) danced with Diaghilev's Ballets Russes; ballet master, star, and choreographer of the Paris Opera. He is the author of a number of books on dance, and his article, taken from Opera, Ballet, Music Hall, *links dance and mime.*

IT IS THE EXPRESSION in the eyes, *the look* which is the most sincere and complete reflection of the soul's recesses. Yet it does not present a mirror to the soul—rather does it project emotion on the outer world, that emotion which precedes action in the making. With an artist, before he can express or translate in gestures what he is feeling—or what is felt by the character he embodies—the expression in the eyes betrays the inner attitude, the instinctive reaction, so to speak, untarnished as yet by any element of conscious speculation.

One look that is *theatrically* wrong is enough to warp the meaning of a play. And on the contrary, the exactitude, from the artistic viewpoint, of the expression in the actor's eyes is one of the essential characteristics the sum total of which makes up the *stage worthiness* of any actor.

The other assets are the face, the figure and the art of the mime; all three play towards the expression-value of the body, which in its own right, and by its own weapons, creates laughter or tears, joy or sorrow. For the true gift of an actor lies in his quality as a mime, affecting both face and body—a feature which draws the comedian and the tragedy actor together to such an extent that the alleged boundaries between the different genres are blurred.

The art of the mime is nothing but the technicality of the spirit and the soul, both the channels through which they assert themselves and the overtones they assume. Thus a step in itself has no meaning; only as it accompanies a fleeting expression on the face or a twitch of the muscles does it accede to the quality of a dramatic act with a given significance—the overtones of action to precede action itself. Chaliapine, Chopin, Pavlova, Nijinski, Raimu, Greta Garbo were all mimes in their respective callings.

In ballet dancing the art of the mime plays a very great role. Is it not the true foundation of the "ballet-as-action" advocated by Noverre? The convention-ridden pantomime of the old theatre we hold very cheap; it consisted of short scenes during which the dancers, clumsily gesticulating like so many deaf-mutes, attempted to thread together the episodes of a non-existing central theme; and the naturalist

111

inspiration of it was only too obvious. There remains the art of the mime—the true mime never falls a prey to realism—emotion is the key for him. His technique knows of no form, since it resides in the innermost recesses.

When Toscanini leads Beethoven's Ninth, he mimes it in his own style, but that sort of a pantomime, reflecting as it does abstract moods of the soul, deliberately parts company with reality, indeed shies away from it . . . . In the same way Horowitz's pantomime spreads even to his fingers which seemingly force the music onto the instrument and pluck it up again. That is what is known as the imprint of the artist.

There is no such a thing as a *school for mime*; it is a gift at birth, a basic power in which the artist's professional technique can be securely anchored.

Life's a Lark
Grock

Grock (1880–1959), Swiss clown, and one of the most famous clowns of circus, stage, and music hall. This excerpt is taken from Life's a Lark.

"WHY DID YOU become a clown?"

"Because I wanted to."

"D'you suppose you'll ever be able to earn a decent living by tight-roping and pulling faces?"

"Oh, yes, I'll be rich one day."

My goal and I were one from the very beginning. My boy's eyes would regard the world simply as a place wherein I might practise my handsprings and efforts on the tightrope. Once, when the noonday traffic was at its height, I balanced myself, feet in air, on the bridge-rail in the Bienne Central Square. The river was in full spate with the recent rains. Innumerable passers-by were seized with horror at the inevitable accident that must ensue, and nothing but the technical skill of the future acrobat rescued him from the peril of those two hundred pairs of arms stretched out for his salvation.

On another occasion I proceeded to school by the most natural of routes—the wire fences fronting the little gardens of the houses that line the river bank. At about a yard from the ground I tightroped along the distance of three-quarters of a mile from the lake into town. I was followed by a bevy of admiring school friends and we all arrived late.

By the following Sunday I was sufficiently far advanced to invite my schoolmates to a show in our bar parlour at the back of the inn. I appeared before them in a get-up reminiscent of the rainbow. The programme opened with a "musical bottle turn"; the bottles were filled with varying degrees of water and then struck with a wooden spoon, each bottle, according to the amount of water it contained, giving out a different tone. I played a Bernese march upon them, and the Marseillaise. After which I initiated my audience into the elementary mysteries of the contortionist's craft, and did splits before them. A violin turn, treated acrobatically, and accompanied by my sister in masterly fashion at the piano, brought the performance to a close amid universal acclamations. I had made my first public appearance.

Umberto Guilleaume, who goes by the name of Antonet, a leading clown of the Cirque de Paris, was my teacher. He comes of a famous Italian clown family. I was the bud, so to say, that burst into bloom beneath the rays of Antonet's sun . . . . I think Antonet and myself

Figure 15. Grock in *Wait, my Lad!* (Photo: Stone, Berlin. Courtesy Arno Press, Inc.)

can justly pride ourselves on having raised the clown's profession to a higher level and made it more respected. We opened up new paths, and showed that the clown can be a great deal more than just Silly Hans, running after the Ring Master in the intervals, bumping his nose into the lights. A good clown, these days, can occupy every bit as high a position as a good actor. He is practising an art.

If I had a hundred lives at my disposal, I'd never want to be anything but a music-hall artiste. There's something about my profession that's irresistible, or so I think—this mastering by will power, this transforming the little, everyday annoyances, not only overcoming but actually *transforming* them into some strange and terrific thing.

Your clown, just as much as any other artist, is the product of tradition. Just as a painter knows how to use the experience of countless forerunners, just as an author who *is* an author largely owes his existence to the pioneer work of those who have gone before and influenced him, so every clown that is worth his salt is but carrying on the torch handed to him by all the eminent clowns who preceded him or who work with him still. Your painter will swear by Raphael, or Calame, or Stuck as the case may be, your author by Paul de Kock, Goethe, or Edgar Wallace, while your clown will acknowledge his debt to Bebe and Serillo, or Pippo and Toniloff, or Toto, or Willi and Adolf Olschonski, or La Water Lee, or Gobert Belling, or Les Briators, or Rico and Alex, or Seiffer, or Carlo and Mariano, or Little Walter, or Averino Antonio, or the three Fratellini, or Antonet.

The Mastery of Movement
Rudolf Laban

Rudolf Laban (1879–1958), teacher and theoretician of mime and movement, invented Labanotation, a system of recording movement. His classification of dance movement is in current use. This excerpt comes from The Mastery of Movement.

THE ART OF THE STAGE developed from mime, which is the representation of inner movements by visible outer motions. Mime is the stem of the tree that has branched into dance and drama. Dance is accompanied by music, and drama by speech. Both music and speech are produced by movements which have become audible.

The theatrical art in which bodily movement is all-important is mime, an art form which is almost unknown in our time. The nearest approach to it was the silent film before the "talkie" came. Mime uses a differentiated language of gesture, a language which can be fairly well translated into words. Mimed dialogues or soliloquies can be understood and verbally described, at least in their essentials.

It is to be expected that mime, as expressive of effort and a fundamental creative activity of man, will, after its long period of neglect, become once more an important factor of civilized progress, when its real sense and meaning have been reacquired. The value of characterization through dancelike mime movements lies in the avoidance of the simple imitation of external movement peculiarities. Such imitation does not penetrate to the hidden recesses of man's inner effort.

A mime often transmits to the spectator what kind of an inner struggle his character is going through solely by his body, carriage or posture without perceptible movement or sound. Even in everyday life it is possible to see in a person's carriage as well as in his movements the way his thinking and feeling goes. It is the mime's task to draw us, his audience, into the world of his drama by his bodily expression and gestures so that we can identify ourselves with the characters and suffer with the suffering, or feel angry with the rightfully indignant, or laugh at our mirrored selves. If we can do this, we have been lifted out of ourselves and removed from the selfish pleasure for the sake of which we often help people or give presents or perform other charitable acts. Although the artist draws for his creation on real-life situations, feelings and actions, these are not directly depicted in his mime but are given significant form out of his own imagination and vision. In this sense the actor can be a great giver of his own self, and become a mediator between the solitary self of the spectator and world of values.

116

The mediating activity of the actor demands veracity in a high degree. The competent actor, mime, or dancer strikingly reveals the possibility of action. It is a great error to regard the theatre and acting as make-believe, and as dealing with false actions and ideals. Mime and the theatre introduce the spectator to the realities of the inner life and the unseen world of values. The attempts to understand the world through naturalism and materialistic realism are doomed to failure. The realities of the inner life can only be depicted by art in which reason and emotion are compounded, and not by intellect or feeling in isolation. To give the right answer to the innermost expectations of the spectator, the actor must master the chemistry of human effort, and he must realise the intimate relationship between that chemistry and the struggle for values of which life consists. Although a spectator might not have any other reason for visiting the theatre than the wish to be entertained, he is nevertheless dissatisfied if he does not glimpse the realities of the world of values, and that world can be effectively depicted only through both external and inner mobility.

My Sense of Drama

Charles Chaplin

Charles Spencer Chaplin (1889-1977), probably the most famous comic actor and mime to date; writer, director and composer. Excerpts from an interview published in Life Magazine.

MY SENSE OF DRAMA lies in what is unspoken—what is beneath the surface of very commonplace, conventional words and actions.

In pantomime, if it's good, you can get away with anything, and make it believable. Movement is near to nature—as a bird flying—and it is the spoken word which is embarrassing. The voice is *so* revealing, it becomes an artificial thing, reducing everybody to a certain glibness, to an unreality. Pantomime to me is an expression of poetry, comic poetry.

Comedy is essentially what just comes out of you. And when this is happening I say to myself, just be very real with this. I remember a scene years ago. Two bearded men sitting at a lunch counter—I have obviously false whiskers and I dip my hands in the other's finger bowl and dry them on his whiskers. It wasn't treated as comedy. It was madness that the audience recognized as madness, but I treated it perfectly normally. The audience feels it is in on something special, something the person on the moving screen isn't. That's the basic element that's in comedy. What appears to be sane is really insane. And if you can make that poignant enough, the audience really loves it.

I never thought of the tramp in terms of appeal. He was myself, a comic spirit, something within me that said I must express this. I felt so free. The adventure of it. The madness. I can do any mad, crazy think I like. And then?—did it come off, this insane idea I had, did it come off? That was the thrill.

The idea of being fastidious, very delicate about everything was something I enjoyed. Made me feel funny. There is that gentle poverty, quiet poverty about all the Cockneys who ape their betters. Every little draper, soda clerk wants to be a swell, dress up. So when I stumbled over some dog's leash, got my hand stuck in a cuspidor, I knew instinctively what to do. I tried to hide it. They yelled—the mere fact that I didn't want anybody to see it.

I think the secret of the tramp was that people recognize the humanity of him. And human beings *are* very funny, especially when placed in an embarrassing situation.

You cannot beat the human equation—the things which open up a picture of humanity as it really is. As the tramp I think I endeared myself through his terrific humility—the humility which I'm sure is a universal thing—of somebody without money.

Perhaps because of my early environment, the comedy in tragedy has always been second nature to me. Cruelty, for example, is an integral part of comedy. We laugh at it in order not to weep.

But I'm not too interested in why people laugh—only that they do.

A lot of my comic business was ad-libbed. If I feel, have emotion, then one is ebullient, effervescent with ideas. I think creation comes initially out of mood—music, a calm sea, a rough sea, a beautiful day —you say, oh God, I want to do something. Creative people are not always languishing about in an ecstasy of creative inspiration. You don't just come down one morning and begin, because the muses don't work that way. You have to open the gates for them by mood.

Then maybe you get a plot, a skeleton, and then you plug away at it every morning to put flesh on it. That is when you need great enthusiasm, that sense of personal discovery—which is the child in all creative artists—suddenly expressing life and finding life.

But I think you're liable to kill your enthusiasm if you delve too deeply into the psychology of the characters you are creating. I don't want to know about the depths; I don't think they're interesting. And motives are always reduced to that banal sex. And so what!

The most important thing is a close-up when somebody smiles or looks at somebody and it is real and it is the end of the world and the beginning of everything.

The fact is, I've never liked the close-up too much, except for very important moments of emphasis and intimacy. I think that's because my early experience in the theater has made me look on the camera lens as a small proscenium in everything I've done. I like the choreography of movement of the theater—the sense of distances, the timing of effective exits and entrances. If I have any rule, it is that I like orientation first—the camera way back—to know where you are. There's more air; it's not stifling.

And you must give time for the illusion to grow, otherwise it loses its reality. It takes time—you put a seed in the ground and it grows. Then you intensify it. You don't start with intensifying it.

Sometimes it comes through with a great deal of magic. I had a close-up—the last scene of *City Lights*. The blind girl has recovered her sight, thanks to a benefactor she always imagined was a rich and handsome young man. And now she touches again the hands of this little tramp—and seeing through her fingers, as it were, it comes down on her. "My God, this is the man." I had had several takes and they were all overdone, overacted, overfelt. This time I was looking more at her, interested to see that she didn't make any mistakes. It was a beautiful sensation of not acting, of standing outside of myself. The key was exactly right—slightly embarrassed, delighted about meeting her again—apologetic without getting emotional about it. He was watching and wondering what she was thinking and wondering without any effort. It's one of the purest inserts—I call them inserts, close-ups—that I've ever done. One of the purest.

I went to Hollywood and Keystone in 1914. I was about twenty-four and looked eighteen, a callow youth and *very* nervous. The first time I wore my tramp costume was in something called *Mabel's Strange Predicament*. The scene was a hotel lobby, a rather comfortable hotel. Here was this very crummy-looking tramp. He walks in doing all the things a man of assurance would do, looking at the register—"Anybody I know?"—tips his hat to the ladies. And what he really wants to do is get anchored on a soft seat and rest awhile. Sore feet and everything else. Takes out a cigaret butt and lights it; watches the passing parade. Pretty ladies trip over his feet, and he raises his hat, says "Very sorry." I became alive, a person in a logical situation. I felt good, I felt right. The character came to me.

In my little studio I built in California, those were some of my happiest moments, creating my own world, a comic world.

Many times bits of business were the outcome of a lot of agony. Miserable days. Nothing going, nothing working. Trying this, trying that, and so forth. And getting more despondent every day. Everybody looking at you and saying, you think of something that will make them laugh. I'd have this fear—will this thing in me last? I'd get a good gag and then I'd say, oh will another one come?

You place yourself in a labyrinth and try to find your way out.

I don't feel like an old man—I enjoy my age because there are a lot of things one gives up, a lot of fears.

What has always sustained me—the place where I have really existed —has been my work. One man summed it up, said a very succinct thing about me: "He cares."

I thought that was a very good summation of the thing that I am. I care about my work. It's the best thing I do. If I could do something else better, I would do it. But I can't, and so this thing that I've got, whatever it is, whether it's creativeness or whatever it is, I care. I really care.

My Wonderful World of Slapstick
Buster Keaton

Buster Keaton (1895–1966) began in vaudeville at age three, and made his first screen appearance in 1917 in a film with Fatty Arbuckle. Excerpted from My Wonderful World of Slapstick.

BEFORE I WAS MUCH bigger than a gumdrop I was being featured in our act, The Three Keatons, as "The Human Mop." One of the first things I noticed was that whenever I smiled or let the audience suspect how much I was enjoying myself they didn't seem to laugh as much as usual. I guess people just never do expect any human mop, dishrag, beanbag, or football to be pleased by what is being done to him. At any rate it was on purpose that I started looking miserable, humiliated, hounded, and haunted, bedeviled, bewildered, and at my wit's end. Some other comedians can get away with laughing at their own gags. Not me. The public just will not stand for it. And that is all right with me. All of my life I have been happiest when the folks watching me said to each other, "Look at the poor dope, wilya?"

I had seen some of Arbuckle's work in Sennett comedies and greatly admired him. He said he's caught our act many times and always liked it.

"Have you ever been in a movie, Buster?" he asked.

When I told him I hadn't, Roscoe said, "Why don't you come over to the Colony Studios tomorrow morning? I'm starting a new picture there. You could try doing a bit in it. You might enjoy working in pictures." "I'd like to try it," I told him . . . .

Everything about the new business I found exciting and fascinating. Incidentally, I've been told that my first scene in *The Butcher Boy* is still the only movie-comedy scene ever made with a newcomer that was photographed only once. In other words my film debut was made without a single retake. The greatest thing to me about picturemaking was the way it automatically did away with the physical limitations of the theatre. The camera had no such limitations. The whole world was its stage. If you wanted cities, deserts, the Atlantic Ocean, Persia, or the Rocky Mountains for your scenery and background, you merely took your camera to them. From the first day on I hadn't a doubt that I was going to love working in the movies.

I could not have found a better-natured man to teach me the movie business, or a more knowledgeable one. We never had an argument. I can only remember one thing he ever said that I disagreed with.

"You must never forget," he told me that day, "that the average mentality of our movie audience is twelve years." I thought that over a long time, for three whole months in fact. Then I said to Roscoe, "I think you'd better forget the idea that the movie audience has a twelve-year-old mind. Anyone who believes that won't be in pictures for very long, in my opinion." I pointed out how rapidly pictures were improving technically. The studios were also offering better stories all of the time, using superior equipment, getting more intelligent directors. "Every time anyone takes another good picture," I said, "people with adult minds will come to see it." On thinking it over, Arbuckle said I was right. But the low estimate of the audience's mind, I notice, survives to this day in Hollywood. I sometimes wonder if TV, free or not, could have overtaken and overwhelmed the movie industry so quickly if its studio bosses had rejected that myth.

I was always puzzled later on when people spoke of the similarities in the characters Charlie and I played in movies. There was, to me, a basic difference from the start: Charlie's tramp was a bum with a bum's philosophy. Lovable as he was he would steal if he got the chance. My little fellow was a workingman and honest. For example, let us say that each wanted a suit he saw in a shop window. Charlie's tramp would admire it, search his pockets, come up with a dime, shrug, and move on, hoping he'd be lucky next day and have the money to buy it. He would steal the money if he couldn't find it any other way. If not, he would forget all about the suit. Though my little man also stopped, admired the suit, and had not the money to buy it, he would never steal to get it. Instead he would start trying to figure out how he could earn extra money to pay for it.

Lloyd's screen character was quite different from both Chaplin's and mine. He played a mama's boy who continually surprised everyone, including himself, by triumphing over an impossible situation and displaying, in fits and starts, the fighting heart of a lion. Often Lloyd seemed more acrobat than comedian. But whatever he was on the screen he always did a lot better than all right.

The only words we had to write were for the title and subtitles. The fewer subtitles we used the better it was for the picture. What made audiences laugh at our silent comedies was what they watched happening on the screen. The sight gags we used served to bring out the absurdity of things, people's actions, the preposterous situations the movie characters got into and had to escape.

In one or two of my later two-reelers I had tried putting in a story line. But this had not always proved feasible, and the faster the gags came in most short comedies, the better. In the features I soon found out that one had to present believable characters in situations that the audience accepted. The best format I found was to start out with a normal situation, maybe injecting a little trouble but not enough to prevent us from getting laughs. That permitted us to introduce the characters getting in and out of situations that were not too difficult. It was when we approached the final third of the picture that we had the characters in serious trouble which permitted bigger laughs, the biggest of all coming when catastrophe threatens. I never repeated a gag or used the same plot twice unless these could be so heavily camouflaged as to be unrecognizable.

Another interesting thing I learned later was that once you got the audience interested in what the hero was doing they deeply resented anything that interrupted him. It didn't matter what terrific gag you gave them. The other gags were accepted by audiences who saw the whole picture, because they did not interfere with my job of saving the girl. But when I directed the submarine traffic I was interrupting the rescue to do something else that couldn't help us out of the jam. From that day on, I realized that my feature comedies would succeed best when the audience took the plot seriously enough to root for me as I indomitably worked my way out of mounting perils.

There was also the matter of timing. Just as in vaudeville, you lost the laugh when you threw a gag at them too quickly, or for that matter too slowly. The difference was that on the stage you had the chance to test and retest your comedy material before live audiences. The customers only saw a gag or comedy scene in a movie after it was made, cut, and in the can. Often it was expensive remaking scenes with brand new gags in them. And that's how the protection or alternate gag was born.

In almost every picture I've made I make it a rule to become very serious about the fourth reel or so. That is to make absolutely sure that the audience will really care about what happens to me in the rest of the picture.

Slapstick comedy has a format, but it is hard to detect in its early stages unless you are one of those who can create it. The unexpected was our staple product, the unusual our object, and the unique was the ideal we were always hoping to achieve.

My World of Comedy
Harold Lloyd

*Harold Lloyd (1893–1971) apprenticed to the stage and as a film
extra before the famed* Safety Last, *1923. This excerpt is taken
from* Harold Lloyd's World of Comedy.

MY AMBITION TO BE an actor goes back to the first time I can remember
knowing what an actor was. I never had any other idea. I began playing
in amateur theatricals. I would spend hours before the mirror making
eyebrows and mustaches with charcoal or anything that would leave a
mark on my small face.

The tools of my trade: the store of knowledge of comedy effects—
what they are and how to obtain them—accumulated by long experience and observation and sharpened by a natural instinct for what is
funny. The comedy is in the humor of events, not in any conscious
effort of mine to be cute. The theater caught me young, and no experience in it—cellar stage, amateur, stock company, stage hand, picture
extra, or one-reel slapstick—was wasted. Specialization, plus aptitude,
plus work, seemed to be the formula for my advancement in the
films. I realize this is not exactly new. But these are the ingredients,
as I study the situation, that have been most helpful to me.

Funny material and knowing what is funny are just a part of the
making of a top-flight comic. Looking funny can get you off to a good
start. But it does not sustain. A top comic must have a knowledge of
pantomime and how to present his comic ideas in an individual
way . . . . It's difficult to put all this into words. But a comedian
must have that certain capacity within himself for funny ideas which
may come to him at any time, even while in the middle of a scene.
Thus he can add to what he is doing, build on it, and render even
funny lines and situations funnier.

The earliest method of comedy construction was to begin with a
policeman or policemen to chase your comedian. The rest of the cast
was optional, except that there must be a girl. We would sometimes
get a general idea, a cast to fit it, and a good location, and then we'd
start shooting. We often started in mid-picture. We couldn't afford gag
men, so Roach and I would usually think up our own ideas. We never
hesitated to stop the progress of the story or to forget about the story
completely in order to shoot a reel of gag sequences. In the early days
it was the gag that came first. We would work for as long as we
thought necessary and then we would quit for a few days until someone got a new idea. Of course, as feature films developed we went far

beyond these early techniques and began utilizing more subtle plots and characterizations.

Frankly, slapstick comedies had created laugh riots for people all over the world, and, when I began to produce pictures of a different kind, it was foolish for me to feel that slapstick was passe. But pictures with a logical basis, a foundation of solid story material, needed to get away from the hodge-podge of slapstick. The audience could not be led to expect one brand of comedy and then be given another. I think the best prescription I can give for success in one type of comedy-producing is to change constantly the type of story in which one appears. Introduce new types of characters and surroundings, and keep your material logical, even though it may stretch the imagination a little. There is a certain formula, but it's not so clear as formulas for baking a cake or making a suit of clothes: one cannot follow a recipe or pursue any set course in laugh-making. What is funny in one situation is incongruous and almost idiotic in another.

There are certain sure-fire situations, but they cannot be used continuously. An idea used in one picture may meet the expected response. But repeated in another, it's bound to be a miserable flop. Public moods are varied and fickle. One time they run to broad slapstick comedy. The next time the more subtle type of fun appeals most. If it cannot hold a mirror up to life, however, a film comedy can keep within shooting distance of verity. The only test it should pass is: 'Is it plausible while one is looking at it?' It will be so only if the characters themselves are plausible. The actions may be outlandish, but the characters, particularly the central character, must not be. Everyone in the audience should feel that he knows him, has known him, or might easily know him.

Comedy demands a technique of its own. The big producers have learned that. They once tried to make funny pictures with dramatic directors and failed. Then they called in former comedy directors who had graduated to the larger field. Most dramatic directors cannot time and space comedy, and actors who are accustomed only to dramatic work move too slowly through comedy scenes and fail to underscore their actions properly. My comedy was basic. There were no language barriers. Take a little boy throwing a snowball at a man and knocking off his top hat—that's basic. Take a fellow slipping on a banana peel—that's basic too.

Of course, one never exactly learns what he shouldn't do, but it pays to notice the sign posts along the way. For example, a comedian is not supposed to let the audience think he believes his comedy is funny. He can't laugh at himself. We occasionally have a great comedian, like Red Skelton, who laughs at his own jokes and gets away with it. But he is the exception. Some people used to say that I was funny because I knew how to construct a gag or a situation. But they overlooked the idea that my Glass Character was inherently funny in the way he thought and the way he reacted. If I ran, I ran with a funny, screwball way to make it funny. If I talked, I did it in my own special way. I was an individual with characteristics all my own. And I had to forego the advantage of a lot of gags because I wanted to retain the consistency of the character I had built up. It was early in the development of my Glass Character that I realized I must not go into a lot of cartoon-type stuff. In other words, I very seldom did a gag that couldn't be done in real life, at least with a stretch of the imagination.

I never took my glasses off. I don't think my audiences ever saw a picture of Harold Lloyd without his glasses. If I was to play a girl, I played a girl with glasses. If I was to play a Civil War soldier, I had my glasses adapted to give the feeling of a century ago. So, when I played football, people didn't give a thought to it that I wore my glasses. Even when I went in swimming, I had my glasses on. When I was in bed, I had them on too. People accepted the glasses as part of my screwball type of character. With them, I was Harold Lloyd. Without them I was a private citizen. I was able to stroll unrecognized down any street in the land at any time without the glasses, a boon granted to few other motion picture actors, and one for which some of them would pay quite well.

Mr. Laurel and Mr. Hardy
Stan Laurel

Laurel and Hardy had appeared in motion pictures separately
before playing together in 1926. These excerpts are taken from
Mr. Laurel and Mr. Hardy.

I DON'T KNOW HOW to answer young comedians who ask me how they
can learn their trade. For one thing, I guess they just don't have the
advantages today that we had. A friend once asked me what comedy
was. That floored me. What *is* comedy? I don't know. Does anybody?
Can you define it? All I know is that I learned how to get laughs, and
that's all I know about it. You have to learn what people will laugh
at, then proceed accordingly. First of all, you should start out, I think,
with a fairly believable plot, no matter how broad it is, and then work
on from there. But you've got to *learn* how to go on from there. Nobody's going to teach you. That's why one of the best ways for a
young comedian to learn his trade is to get as much summer stock as
possible, appearing in repertory, changing parts, being in different
situations, over and over again until he learns the "feel" of different
audiences. He has to learn why certain gags go over, and why they
don't. You develop an intuition after facing various types of audiences.
What one will laugh at, another won't, and vice versa. One day you'll
know. Then, you're in business.

[On the pie sequence in *The Battle of the Century*] We come to a
bakery shop with a pie wagon standing in front. Hardy drops the peel
for me on the sidewalk there, and the pieman comes along with a big
tray of pies, and slips on the peel. He's covered with pies. As he clears
his eyes, he happens to see Hardy pushing the banana into my hand,
and realizes that Hardy is trying to put the blame on me. An argument
starts, ending up with the pieman pushing a pie in Hardy's face. I resent this and push a pie in the *pieman's* face. Hardy laughs at this and
the guy instead of hitting me back hits Hardy with another pie. At
this point, a stranger passing by tries to stop the argument, and gets
the pie in the face, too. Gradually, one by one, other people get into
the argument until finally the entire street, a full block, is pie-crazy.
Everybody is pie-throwing happy. The camera goes up to take a panorama view of all these people throwing, throwing, throwing. There are
pies thrown into a dentist's office, in windows, out of them. Nothing
but pies—thousands of them. Then a cop who, of course, is all covered
with pie arrests us and is taking us away, but *he* slips on the banana
peel—and he falls down a manhole for the finish.

We never tried to use funny clothing. Of course, there were times when we would wear odd garments for a special humorous effect, but as far as our two characters were concerned, we never tried to get very far from what was real. We always wore a stand-up collar but there wasn't anything unreal about them, especially in the twenties and early thirties. Stand-up collars were formal and slightly different but never too obviously so. They gave us, together with our derbies, a something we felt these two characters needed—a kind of phony dignity. There's nothing funnier than a guy being dignified *and* dumb. As far as make-up goes, I emphasized my lack of brains by making my face as blank as possible. I used very light make-up and made my eyes small by lining the inner lids. Babe, in keeping with his wish to obtain an even *bigger* kind of dignity, combed his hair down in a spit-curl bangs effect. This was in perfect harmony with his elegant nature and those fancy-dan gestures of his.

We had a rough idea of schedule, but our prime worry was whether or not the picture was going to be good. The studio didn't bother us much if at all about a schedule because we didn't have a lot of people in our casts as a rule. There weren't any unions, and people just worked until we got the effects we wanted. Sometimes we would have a change in a gag situation that called for alteration of the set. So we'd wait a couple of days until it was rebuilt. That takes time. We really didn't have any idea of how precisely long it would take us to do a film. It really depended on the kind we were doing. If we were doing both day and night exterior shots on the same set we would sometimes keep going right through the day and then on all that night until the following morning. This, of course, was when we felt like going ahead on a spurt to finish the picture. It got pretty rough at times especially if we were making water scenes. You can get pretty tired working all night soaking wet as we did on many occasions. As for the times between pictures, that always varied. After the picture was assembled, we previewed it and if no retakes were needed, we started to prepare the next story. That would generally take three or four weeks, sometimes more, sometimes less. Years later, more time was taken on the feature films, of course. If [Hal] Roach was anxious for us to get started, we'd go into production almost right away after finishing a picture, and complete the script as we went along. We would start out with an idea, go along working on it as we were shooting, and then we would frequently deviate from the original idea. We worked hard, but there was no real pressure. It was fun, particularly in the silent days. If something went wrong with what we were doing, we'd just "cut" and laugh about it. Then we'd talk it over and go on shooting. It was damned fine fun and damned hard work in those days when we were making ourselves a well-known team. Come to think of it, it was always fun.

Figure 16. Bert Williams in a vaudeville sketch. (Courtesy Archives for the Performing Arts, San Francisco.)

Bert Williams, Everybody
Bert Williams

*Bert Williams (1875–1922), America's first pantomime star,
played in every popular medium. As a light-skinned immigrant
from the British West Indies, he had to learn and assume the black
racial stereotype in make-up and language. These excerpts are
taken from his biography* Nobody *by Ann Charters.*

IN TRUTH, I HAVE never been able to discover that there was anything
disgraceful in being a colored man. But I have often found it inconvenient—in America.

Truly, it seemed that I was and am still constantly storing away
dialects and little bits of mimicry, together with mental pictures. One
day at Moore's Wonderland in Detroit, just for a lark, I blacked my
face and tried the song "Oh, I Don't Know, You're Not So Warm."
Nobody was more surprised than I was when it went like a house on
fire. Then I began to find myself. It was not until I was able to see
myself as another person that my sense of humor developed.

One of the funniest sights in the world is a man whose hat has been
knocked in or ruined by being blown off—provided, of course, it be
the other fellow's hat! All the jokes in the world are based on a few
elemental ideas, and this is one of them. The sight of other people in
trouble is nearly always funny. This is human nature. If you will observe your own conduct whenever you see a friend falling down on
the street, you will find that nine times out of ten your first impulse
is to laugh and your second is to run and help him get up. To be polite
you will dust off his clothes and ask him if he has hurt himself. But
when it is all over you cannot resist telling him how funny he looked
when he was falling. The man with the real sense of humor is the
man who can put himself in the spectator's place and laugh at his own
misfortunes.

Where I got the idea for my pantomime poker game: . . . There was
one fellow in a [hospital] room alone. Evidently his mental illness was
due to gambling, playing poker. In his room was a table and chair.
He was there all alone, talking to himself and acting as though he
were in a poker game, for he would go through the motions of having
a drink, looking around the table and smiling at the other players. He
would reach in his imaginary pile of chips and throw in his ante, looking around to see if everybody was in, then smile again. He would
shuffle and begin to deal around and after he finished dealing, he
would pick up his imaginary hand and look at each player after they

had discarded, to see how many cards they wanted. All this time he would have a smile on his face as if he believed he had the best hand, and as each player asked for cards his smile would get broader. As each imaginary player would ask for cards he would put up fingers to show he understood how many. Then when one of the imaginary players stood pat, his smile would suddenly begin to vanish. When the deal was all over, the betting would start. Each player would call or pass. When it was up to him he would look at his hand, put it down, pour a little drink from his imaginary bottle and look again. Then he would push in the last of his chips and call.

Figure 17. Angna Enters in *Boy Cardinal.* (Photo: Toppo, New York, from Angna Enters, *First Person Plural*, 1937. Courtesy Stackpole Books.)

Mime is a Lonely Art

Angna Enters

Angna Enters (b. 1907) was a painter, dancer, mime, writer, composer, teacher; she also wrote film scenarios and directed plays. Enters was the first American concert mime, predating the French mime wave by several years. Her article was first published in Angna Enters: On Mime.

MIME IS A LONELY art, for the mime works in a solitary world inhabited by phantasms which take only transient physical form through him.

Anything extraneous to their will—such as an attempt by the mime to draw attention to himself by signals to the audience that he, like them, appreciates the foibles of his characters—causes these creatures to withdraw in a sulk, and the mime discovers himself stranded with only his own ego for company. At that moment when he feels obliged to step out of his character to communicate personally with the audience, he pays the heavy penalty of becoming estranged from the figures of his imagined world and of being forsaken by the audience.

I can illustrate this by an experience I once had. Some of my performances were given in rural communities where I was the first "live" performer the audience had seen except for a few instrumentalists and singers, not to mention local student productions of the then ubiquitous *Kiss and Tell*, an already passé Broadway hit.

At two consecutive such performers, the audience seemed perplexed at what I was doing until the second or third number. I thought I would try to gain a more immediate response by slight exaggerations of glances or movements, in an effort to communicate with the audience more quickly. While these actions aroused audible signs of life, I soon realized that they had nothing to do with understanding of the character, but were only taken as an indication to the audience that I was on their side rather than in sympathetic and sustained accord with the figure performed.

I remember distinctly saying to myself after the second try, while changing into the third costume, "After this I will mind my own business!"

This proved good advice, for I found out, from later comments, that what I had believed to be a failure of the audience to respond in the manner I expected was, in fact, only their concentration on what I was doing; they were enjoying a gradual awakening—a slow transference of their understanding from their own time and place to those which appeared so unexpectedly before their eyes. This was evidenced by their growing response to succeeding numbers. In that sense,

133

audiences are not unlike visitors to a foreign land who discover that the modes, manners, and thought of its inhabitants are not meaningless oddities, but are sensible in context.

Mime opens up a new world to the beholder, but it does so insidiously, not by purposely injecting points of interest in the manner of a teacher or tour guide. The mime is no more than the physical medium —the instrument on which the figures of his imagination play their dance of life. He, or she, is a lonely figure in whom neither the audience nor the figures of their imagination have any interest. As in any of the creative arts, the viewer is concerned only with the results of the invention.

To me, the realization of this loneliness is an asset, for it provides a sense of that isolation in which one is free to abandon oneself to the expression of those images with which one is obsessed.

But the audience for mime also has responsibilities—it must be an alert collaborator. It cannot sit back, mindlessly complacent, and wait to have its emotions titillated by mesmeric musical sounds or visual rhythms or acrobatic feats, or by words which tell it what to think. Mime is an art which, paradoxically, appeals both to those who go to a theatre or circus free to respond instinctively to whatever they see, and to those with sophisticated, whetted perceptions. Between these extremes lie those audiences conditioned to resist any collaboration with what is played before them; and these the mime must seduce despite themselves. There is only one way to attack those reluctant minds—take them unaware! They will be delighted at an unexpected pleasure.

Random Remarks

Charles Weidman

Charles Weidman (1901–1975) helped to establish dance and mime as a recognized combination, although he is looked upon primarily as a dancer. His essay comes from an anthology, The Dance Has Many Faces.

CLARITY AND UNDERSTANDABILITY has remained the basis of my dance creations. Their intent, concerned with human values and the experience of our times, must be carried by the fullest emotional impact the artist can muster. Then, with the conception of the idea, the intelligibility of its message and the emotional intensity of presentation, the artist's primordial task is fulfilled and—however his artistic deliverance may be judged—his sincerity cannot be doubted.

Some may say that I am going too far when I desire to make my dance creations as easily understandable as a movie. But this may explain why more and more I have come to believe in the pantomimic dance drama. The word "pantomime" does not mean to me the presentation of a dumb show, as most dictionaries define it, or the mere telling of a story or action without the use of explanatory words. To me it is the transport of an idea into movement, the animation of the feeling behind the idea, an animation in which suddenly all commas and periods, all silent moments of an unwritten play become a reality in movement. Moreover, it may be likened to that emotional sequence of a growing world of images which we may experience when listening to a symphony, full of logical continuity and expressiveness where words might seem feeble and music inadequate.

I may be prejudiced in favor of the pantomimic dance, because I have found that my gift as a dancer is essentially tied up with my dramatic talent as an actor, or—let us better say—as a mime. The modern mime must be a modern dancer, and as such his entire body must be alive. This cannot be acquired by emotional experience, only by hard physical training. It may be best called bodily awareness. I went so far as to exclude the face, i.e., the facial expression, completely from the pantomimic presentation.

Any idea being projected produced its specific movement and gesture pattern which is, in itself, purely abstract. Though, basically, pantomime is not mere storytelling, a story may be, and usually is, achieved by what is done. But to attain such ends, the means must be determined by strict form, since form alone leads to artistry.

Figure 18. Charles Weidman and Company in *The Unicorn in the Garden.* (Courtesy Charles Weidman.)

In seeking to reach my audience and to convey my message in the easiest understandable manner, I often chose the channels of humor. There are various kinds of humor, but first and foremost it must be said that, whenever a humorous element is required, it can come only from the performer himself and must be projected by him.

In the beginning I employed the most obvious humor, the sadistic type of humor, the effect of which is almost guaranteed with every audience. However, with time, I was continually looking for a broader expression of what I wanted to achieve, and I attempted to abstract the essence of any emotion projected through movement. Here is an example. Instead of being frantic as, let us say, a minstrel would be when a bucket of water is thrown over him, I tried to convey the same idea without impersonating a minstrel and with no bucket of water causing the emotion. This attempt finally crystallized into a dance called *Kinetic Pantomime*. In this composition I so juggled, reversed and distorted cause and effect, impulse and reaction that a kaleidoscopic effect was created without once resorting to any literary representation.

It has been a long and arduous way from this comedy pantomime to Thurber's *Fables*. But my basic approach to subject matter, though it has widened and developed, has never changed. Content and form are equally important to my choreographic pantomimes. I have never believed that artistry can be achieved without adhering to the strictest form, nor that the heart of the public can be reached, if the artist is blind to the life that surrounds him or tries to shut himself off from it by escaping into mere fantasy and romance. Art demands that we be part of life and merge with it. Art and life are as indivisible an entity as the artist and his audience.

Figure 19. Red Skelton in his clown character. (Courtesy Red Skelton.)

I'll Tell All

Red Skelton

Red Skelton (b. 1913) was among the first to perform pantomime on TV, 1950. Like many of the early film comics, he had a long career in vaudeville, nightclubs, circuses, and medicine shows before coming to motion pictures and TV. These excerpts are taken from an early autobiographical series published in the Milwaukee Journal.

AT THE RIPE OLD age of twelve, already a veteran of a medicine show and a minstrel troupe, I was playing a Missouri River showboat. However, in the interest of truth I must say that though the range of my performances was wide, the quality was low, as the showboat skipper emphasized one day when I fell into the river. He promptly pitched my clothes and valise in after me, shook his heavy cane in threatening gestures and called in loud and convincing tones that he hoped I drowned, but if I didn't just to keep going away from there until it would take at least a month for a postal card to reach him.

That was a distressing fall, but it wasn't my first, nor my last. I've been falling around, mostly into difficulties, since an extremely early period in life. It was in fact, on my tenth birthday that I fell—literally —into my first role as a thespian. That was with the medicine show.

The show set up for business in a vacant lot in our town and I was fascinated. Seeking out the Doc I told him I'd like to join his enterprise. "What can you do?" he asked, looking me up and down from the top of my red head to the soles of my large but ragged shoes. "I can play a guitar and sing," I said. "Go ahead," he snapped, indicating the assembled throng. But they, like the showboat captain later, were unappreciative. "My boy," said the Doc, "you've misinformed me. Try selling medicine." He pushed a load of bottles into my arms and I rushed through the crowd. As I scrambled back up the steps to the little stage my feet skidded and I took a nose dive into the dust. That brought applause, and from it I took my cue. I went on falling for crowds—and if you'll pardon a little boasting—they've been falling for me nigh onto seventeen years now, with several notable and sad exceptions.

The career which got away that day to such a flying start off the steps has taken me through most of the bypaths of the entertainment world—medicine shows, showboats, stock companies, minstrel shows, burlesque, vaudeville, radio and the movies—and into some

surprising situations, both at work and at play. I've done most everything but Shakespeare and that, I fear, is an ambition destined to
go unfulfilled.

I practiced on my guitar and warbled my songs until I was an integral part of the Doc's performance, especially the afterpieces when we
went in for dramatic and humorous skits like "Over the River,
Charlie" and "The Phone Booth." But I felt the call of the drama and
left the Doc for the John Lawrence Stock Company, doing one night
or more stands through Illinois, Indiana and adjacent states. I was all
of thirteen by this time and went in for old men parts. All painted up
and with a creak in my voice I'd portray anything from a stalwart
farmer of fifty to an old broken down roue of ninety. But Stout's
minstrels crossed my path and I deserted the drama for blackface, and
became a rollicking end man. My favorite number was "Picking Petals
Off Daisies" and with my guitar and song and dance routine I still
can amuse my friends with throwbacks to minstrel days.

Then Hitner's showboat, "Cotton Blossom," hove into view on the
Missouri River. The showboat was quite a business enterprise too.
Wherever we'd tie up we'd trade advertising space for tickets, meats,
vegetables and groceries. No trades, no food, except what we could
get from the river. I thereupon decided to go in for burlesque. For a
couple of years, when I was fourteen and fifteen, I played the best
known burlesque houses over a big circuit, including Indianapolis,
Kansas City, Buffalo, Toronto, South Bend, St. Louis and Chicago. I
was the youngest full-fledged alleged comic in the business.

[After a long, dry period] came the light. At an audition at the Roxy
Theatre all was quiet except for a girl named Eve Rose. She laughed
at my clowning and signed me to emcee a show at the Lido club in
Montreal. That was something new for me; in fact, I don't think I'd
ever been in a night club. But right then I'd have fought a cageful of
tigers for a sandwich if it included coffee. My lucky star started to
shine. Signed for a week, I stayed six at the Lido and one night, Harry
Anger, at Loew's Montreal theater, looked in on my act. He put me in
the theater and I stayed twenty-six weeks, record for the house.

But pride leads to a fall, and at my next stop, the State theater in
Chicago, I fell with a thump that should have been heard around the
world. I've never known why, but my act smelled so bad that they're
still burning incense in the balcony. To make it all the more puzzling,
I moved over to the Stratford in the same city and went over like a
four-alarm fire. That's show business. From Montreal I went to Shea's
theater in Toronto and then shuttled back and forth between Toronto
and Montreal. Then came the merry-go-round: the Palace in Chicago,

etc., etc., until Gene Ford booked me with top billing at Loew's Capitol in Washington.

Gene had put on an advance campaign building me up as a glamor boy until I don't know what Washington expected, but I certainly was not it, especially when I went out right off the bat and fell into the orchestra pit. However, the critics were kind. They said I was no heartbreaker but I was funny. That satisfied me. The wheels of fortune were spinning like a top now. I eventually put in fifty-two straight weeks in vaudeville as a headliner in the country's biggest houses, including New York, and I think that's a record, at least for the last ten years. And right now I'm carrying around about fifty weeks of vaudeville contracts in my pocket. I'm taking no chances on this movie business . . .

VIII. Mime in the Twentieth Century: Contemporary

The line of a design is not the imitation of the lines of the object, but rather the trace of a gesture that seizes and expresses the form.
—Alain

Art, especially comic art, is often something done before it is something thought.
—Walter Kerr

Western art is all action. Eastern art is about what happens between actions.
—Mamako

In a world gone mad, who has more to say to us than the zanies?
—Carlo Mazzone-Clementi

Film is the art of creating illusion through reality, while mime is the art of creating reality through illusions.
—Marcel Marceau

THE PROCESS CONTINUES, with increasing momentum through the 1960s and 1970s. Mime is definitely in, as indicated by the establishing in 1973 of a professional organization—International Mimes and Pantomimists, Marceau's annual tours of the world, the two-year-plus Broadway run by the Mummenschanz, and the appearance of two publications: the *Mime Journal* in 1974 and *Mime, Mask and Marionette* in 1978. International festivals proliferate: beginning in 1962, one or more national or international festivals have been held in Berlin, Zurich, Prague, Frankfurt, Avignon, Morocoo, Strasburg, Cologne, London, Toronto, LaCrosse, and Milwaukee.

At such close range it is impossible to evaluate movements or draw conclusions. What can be seen at present is that the range of mime is ever-widening. At first, as was to be expected, Marceau's impact resulted in many young imitators following in his wake, with the outer forms intact (white face, imaginary objects, short anecdotes) but too often with a lack of inner conviction, or even a sense that the form was a synthesis of some inner working-out. Some earlier nontraditional styles, such as those of Paul Curtis's American Mime Theatre (starting in 1952) and the dance-mimes Enters and Weidman, had been seen prior to Marceau but not nearly so widely; mainly in New York in the case of the first, and by concert audiences in the case of the second. Marceau, however, in addition to the great effect of his artistry, was also seen by millions via television, films, and concerts, thereby stimulating and influencing greater numbers of young artists.

Then some changes in style became manifest. European mimes were exploring new forms, and some of them were seen in the United States for the first time at the 1974 festival in LaCrosse. By the 1978 Milwaukee festival, approximately half of the American performers used traditional French pantomime techniques. The other half had moved out into clowning, or were employing only a few of the traditions, combining them with nontraditional elements like full-length pieces, or real props, or text. Or they incorporated mime into a larger frame of total theatre, using text, dance, narration, mime, mask, clowning, puppets, filmed projections, or any other techniques in varying combinations.

Mime as part of total theatre is not new. As shown in the notes about Asian theatre (p. 41) mime is so integrated into those forms that it scarcely exists as a separate part of Asian drama. In Europe and the United States there have been notable companies and/or productions in which mime was an important feature: San Francisco Mime Troupe since 1959, Bread and Puppet Theatre since 1961, El Teatro Campesino since 1965, National Theatre of the Deaf since 1967, Barrault's

Rabelais, 1968, the 1971 production of *1789* by the Théâtre du Soleil, and the work of Dario Fo and his co-workers since the mid-1960s. Now more and more mime troupes are expanding along similar lines.

The current mime scene also includes political mime. El Teatro Campesino and Bread and Puppet Theatre emerged from a need to deal with political issues: prounion, and antiwar; and Dario Fo's communal theatre is revolutionary in outlook, to name only a few.

In this heretofore largely male art, women mimes are greater in number than ever before. They are members of mime companies, some of them heads of troupes; they are also soloists, such as Mamako, Goslar, and Pinok and Matho.

*   *   *

Here, then, is a temporary stopping place in the presentation of mimes on miming. The current popularity of the art shows no sign of decline and many eager young performers continue to dedicate themselves to the movement art—I say "movement art" for the term "mime" will continue to change its meaning and may even fall away if it should restrict the exploration and growth which must take place. Whatever form it takes, the art of meaningful movement will never cease to enchant, exalt, and amuse.

Figure 20. Marcel Marceau as Bip. (Courtesy Ronald A. Wilford Associates, Inc.)

The Adventure of Silence

Marcel Marceau

Marcel Marceau became a student of Decroux in 1944; he presented his first mimodrama in 1946, and his famous character Bip was born in 1947. In addition to his actual works. Marceau also created an audience for mime. Before him it had been a small part of the theatre-going public—itself a small segment of the population— that attended mime performances. Marceau also writes and paints, and has published several books containing his drawings. This excerpt is taken from Marcel Marceau ou L'aventure du Silence.

THE PANTOMIMES OF style? I begin my program with them so as to acquaint the public with mime. In a way it is a lesson; they are studies of movement in the same way that a pianist plays rather difficult Chopin études. If you look at the sketches of an artist you can see that he is also technically very skillful: look at Ingres or Tiepolo.

In my style pantomimes I see three stages. I began with the identification of man with the elements: Fire, water, air, wind. *The Staircase, Tug-of-War, Optical Illusion, Against the Wind* were techniques of Decroux as applied by Marceau; they are more or less pure exercises of virtuosity. Then further pieces like *The Dice Players* and *At the Clothier's* were personal sketches which could display that virtuosity in a dramatic or comical way.

In *The Public Garden* I created the transitions of characters: from a young man to an old man, from an old man to a soldier, a nurse, child, balloon-vendor, statue—done in a manner quite my own which I call *le retournement du personnage.* In *Youth, Maturity, Old Age and Death* I created birth, life and death of man in four minutes. Time was condensed; it was the most elliptical way of expressing the Seven Ages of Man. Going back to the previous exercises, *The Tightrope Walker* was a dramatic piece showing metaphysical anxiety through the illusion of "seeing" the man ten metres above the floor, while in actuality he is on the ground. In addition, I recreated the visible-invisible and the *point d'appui dans l'espace,* giving the impression of leaning upon something; in reality it is empty space. That phase is completed with *The Mask-Maker*, The Cage*,* and *Contrasts. The Mask-Maker* is in the tradition of the "Grimaciers du Roy." It has become a classic pantomime in which an artisan plays with seven masks. One of them clings to his face, and he cannot take it off—and

---

*Based on an idea by Alexandre Jodorofsky.

Figure 21. Marcel Marceau in a style pantomime. (Courtesy Ronald A. Wilford Associates, Inc.)

here one encounters Baudelaire who was haunted by the symbolism of the mask; one can also find Victor Hugo with *The Man Who Laughs*. What I want to say in this pantomime is that all of us wear several masks, but there is one in which we are revealed one day, at the moment of death, at the moment of truth. My maker of masks tears off the laughing mask and finds himself flayed, with the face of solitude.

In *The Cage* the eye recreates what does not exist. That cage is made of glass; it shows a space in which man is prisoner of solitude, which limits his liberty. He is condemned in advance, and if he succeeds in breaking out, it is only to find himself in another, larger, cage—which then shrinks. Corridors, labyrinths loom up; Kafka's world closes in on him. We create our own cage; it is up to us to break out of it—and anyhow, life stretches between two extremes, birth and death. And all philosophy derives from that inevitable source. In the pantomime, virtuosity plays a large part, for we have to create the nonexistent walls; we have to make solid the thin air.

Contrasts reveals all that man is confronted with between twenty and forty years of age. The action unfolds like a newsreel which shifts from one situation to another like a lap-dissolve; a man dies, another marries, one is shot, another goes to a dance. Like a chameleon, the action changes from one state to another in a series of bodily variations.

The third stage is the present phase. I tend more and more toward allegory, toward abstraction, with *The Hands* (struggle between Good and Evil), *The Creation of the World, Light and Shadow*. In this third stage, the style pantomimes represent the elliptical mime that I have become.

The style pantomimes display all the symbolism regarding man: man-god, man-animal, or simply man, caught between dream and reality, life and death. Because they are played by a character wishing to represent his fellow men, I keep the white mask and the white costume; with that color there is a kind of neutralness, a purity.

Bip is a wan, unearthly, moonlike personage, mouth torn by a red dash and circumflexes over the eyes; little brother of Charlie, grandchild of Pierrot. He is also a sort of Don Quixote who tilts at windmills, an adventurous rogue. The audience identifies with Bip when he is a hero; with him, they take revenge, they are carried along with the emotional outburst ending in the kick in the pants which they themselves would like to be able to give to others. But there is also a certain cruelty on the part of the public, laughing at their own misadventures. Bip is only a symbolic character to the extent that a man becomes a symbol for mankind. In *Bip Hunts Butterflies*, the quivering of the butterfly is that of the heart; the butterfly that flies away is love that fades away. *Bip as a China Salesman* is man at grips with fragile objects. *Bip at a Society Party* is a social satire. *Bip as a Soldier*, an antiwar piece, is an aspect of the Good Soldier Schweik, when all one's wits are employed in the struggle against buttons, against a helmet too big or too small, against a kind of nonsense that ends in war and mud, and in the realization of the absurdity of death in a useless war.

Bip is humanity, but he can also personify legendary and mythical personages. Bip is you and me. At twenty he would look to the heavens, the wide-eyed poet. Since I don't want him to age, I will preserve him on the screen. And when I organize a company, when I create new works to show that mime is not only the expression of a single man, then only Bip, among the other characters of the pieces, will wear a white mask.

Pantomime being explicit, it is necessary to choose distinct subjects, linked by an action. What cannot be expressed is fallacy or ambiguity. Gesture to "explain," that is a mongrel sort of pantomime. For example, one cannot mime "This is not my mother, she is my mother-in-law." To say that, one uses a placard. Or better still, one eliminates the mother-in-law! Dialogue is not within our range. But what one can express very well in mime is: death; or passing intermediary states like love, dreams, hunger, thirst; transitions up to their final outcome. Also contrasting states: dream-reality, love-hate, wealth-poverty, suffering-joy; dimensions, metaphysical anguish, identifications with the elements, tragedy and comedy born of conflicts with society.

Our time has made our art form; it is becoming more elliptical, the anecdote is receding. People understand more quickly, which explains sometimes the great success of the style pantomimes compared to certain anecdotal Bip numbers.

Nevertheless the one-man show characters have achieved their own identity, and they are part of our so complex world of mime which represents the essence of man's vision in a timeless time.

Figure 22. Jacques Lecoq. (Courtesy Jacques Lecoq.)

Mime, Movement, Theatre

Jacques Lecoq

Jacques Lecoq is the fourth of the French four stemming from Copeau's work (see p. 91). He came to mime through sports, then joined the school and company of Jean Dasté, who had worked with Copeau. Lecoq taught and choreographed in Italy for a time, at Padua's University Theatre and the Piccolo Theatre of Milan, where he instituted their physical training program, and elsewhere. In 1956 he founded his present school in Paris. Lecoq sees mime as pre-eminently a research art, for "in that common mimetic source the artist prepares for his choice of thrusts toward different forms of expression." This article appeared in yale/ theatre.

OFTEN PEOPLE ASK me, "What is it you do in your school, is it mime?"

I always feel that the one who asks that question limits the school to wordless formalism. The word "mime" already is restricting. One sees a performer who does not speak and who makes stylized gestures to show imaginary objects, or makes faces to have you understand that he laughs or cries.

Then I answer that I don't do mime, not that kind.

For me, the mime to be learned at the school is at the root of all man's expressions, whether gestural, constructed, modeled, sonorous, written, or spoken. That mime which I call fundamental is the greatest school of the theatre; it is based on movement.

It is in the gesture behind the gesture, in the gesture behind the word, in the movement of material objects, in sounds, colors, and lights, that the school finds its origins. Man understands that which moves by his ability to "mimic" it; that is, to identify himself with the world by re-enacting it with his entire being. Beginning in the silent body of man the impulses toward expression take shape—dramatic impulse and then dramatic creation.

The fire that I look at blazes within me. I can know that fire by identifying with it in action; I give my fire to that fire. The impressions of the body give life to words. But if, when the words leave the body they wander about, comfortably defined, they then harden and die, bearing only emptiness.

Therefore our approach begins with the body.

The school offers a two-year program during which time the student meets challenges and experiments in various theatrical directions at differing levels of dramatic play. By these means he determines where he is, becomes aware of his possibilities, and allows total freedom to his individual creativity. Thus the school opens onto different kinds of theatre, but always theatre linked to the fundamental movement values that students will have learned by observation, and relearned by mimic enactment.

Students do not come unprepared to the school. Many already have some theatre experience, some preconceived ideas, some fixed opinions. At the outset we must unlearn what we know, in order to put ourselves in a state of not-knowing and thereby be available to rediscover what is elemental. We no longer see what is right next to us: a plant, a tree, water, a horse—that which does not change with changing fashion.

The first year is given to unlearning all preconceived ideas, to making the student's body, mind, and senses receptive, and to the recognition of life as it is through daily observation. One does not yet speak of theatre, only of what lives around us. We re-enact people, elements, animals, plants, trees, colors, lights, material objects, sounds; going beyond their images we take cognizance, through improvisations, of their space, their rhythms, and their breathing. We analyze man's physical efforts: his walks, advances, acrobatics, everything he does in order to move and to evolve. The push and pull that makes us what we are. We try to feel that when an arm is raised, it creates in us a corresponding dramatic state, and that an attitude of the body is related to an internal attitude of mind.

Analysis of movement of physical actions, economically done (the least effort for the maximum result), and the neutral dramatic state (being responsive to the present, without past or passion), enable us to better understand how life manifests itself, to remain in a state of permanent discovery, without preconceptions or projections of personal conflicts.

We recall our past situations, forgotten memories, we project our dreams, our make-believe. We study passions and conflict situations so as to grasp their essence and dynamic laws. The bodily *impression* is more important than the bodily *expression.* From all this, and with knowledge of the facts, the student can define that which one day will be his choice, his style, his unique and privileged position in the remaking of the world.

The second year offers him various dramatic directions and a range of creative levels, from the everyday to the symbolic. It is like a series of open windows, in a framework of performance and theatrical communication.

The school offers an approach to knowledge through various courses, not placed end to end but interrelated to each other so that they progress simultaneously in coherent order, and presented by teaching which is linked to the professional careers for which the school prepares its students. And linked at the same time to the knowledge of life that comprises its constant search. Theatre, mime, dance, film, and other forms of human expression will be the means, chosen according to each one's vocation, of creating rapport between the artist and the world.

We address ourselves to the student as creator, and not as interpreter of a defined principle of art. However, certain forms of theatre that I call "maximum" [limites] serve as an example, not for their museum aspect but for the scope that they offer, so that the student can become familiar with a maximum level of theatrical play employing the human being in his entirety. They will serve him as a point of reference. Thus, commedia dell'arte wherein the action is the act, and Greek tragedy wherein the speech is the substance: these are theatre forms which engage the whole being: pelvis, solar plexus, and head.

We use masks a great deal: the neutral mask (without past, without passion to begin with); expressive [character] masks; grotesque masks; and larval masks. They allow one to search for the pivotal point within an action, within a conflict; allow one to find the essential, the gesture that will epitomize the many gestures of daily life, the word of all words. All that is great tends toward immobility [immobility is also a gesture].

Word and gesture are explored from the point where they are merged. A word must be charged with the impression of the body, and not defined by itself.

Pantomime blanche, wherein the gesture replaces the word, offers a study of language. There we try to find again the Roman mimes and mime of the nineteenth century (Deburau) in that storehouse of decadent periods in which only the virtuoso survived.

For several years the study of clowns has taken on larger importance in the school, not in the sense of the traditional circus, which is dead, but in searching out the ridiculous in man. The clown in the spirit of today has replaced the hero, who no longer exists in the theatre. We emphasize the exploration for one's own clown, the one who has grown up within us and which society does not permit us to express. It is total freedom, where the individual can be himself, only himself; it also offers the experience of solitude, a basic experience necessary to understanding the concept of the Chorus. It is very difficult in our time to convey the idea of Chorus, to develop a group to this level [of thinking, acting together]—difficult because of the lack of heroes. The solitude of clowns can help to link the two.

To complete the work, the student will have two experiments to carry out: that of writing, and that of music—always starting from the physical experience—and he will search for a language in which to cast his creation. Then he will leave . . . .

The Cinema According to Tati

Jacques Tati

Jacques Tati, former music hall mime, was first an athlete. His rugby, tennis, and boxing influenced his pantomimes when he began appearing before the public. Tati filmed a series of shorts; his first feature, Jour de Fête, *1949, won prizes, as did* Mr. Hulot's Holiday *and* My Uncle. *Tati writes, directs, and stars in his films. These comments are excerpted from* Jacques Tati.

ONE DOESN'T ALWAYS know why one follows a profession. But it's important to do it oneself. Perhaps I'll make mistakes, maybe big ones, but I'll make them myself. With better technique there wouldn't have been the elementary faults that there were in *Jour de Fête;* the plot would have been more important and well-constructed, but neither would there have been that little detail of the bicycle. I had to write big, in general terms, a postcard technique that might appeal to foreign countries.

I walk around the streets and I always take lots of notes in a little book. But once the character is created, I find his own gags; all of Hulot's gags were foreseen beforehand. I don't much believe that one can find the gags during the shooting. Hulot's gags should come about without his noticing it, without winking to the audience as Chaplin does, without seeming to say: just see what use I can make of the situation. The spectator perhaps admires more the guy who finds the gag on the spot.

One has to know what not to do. Outside of that, it's not so much a question of technique. One must follow the circumstance and one's inspiration. One shouldn't be scornful of the public. They have good taste and good sense, much more than certain ones who maintain the contrary. The public welcomes films that aim to entertain without looking down on it.

First of all I work on my characters. I create them. Then I have them evolve in their settings. I learn to know them better. Take Mme Arpel, the wife of the industrialist. When she wipes the keyhole of the car door with a dust cloth, one should feel that she would at the same time wipe the inside of her husband's ear. And so on with all my characters. Once I have them I no longer work alone. I bring in one or more collaborators—we exchange ideas. We think out loud. That takes time. Having found our characters and our situations, we go on to the making of models of the settings. The work is carried out in collaboration with Jacques Lagrange, but also with the designer

154

Pierre Etaix. The continuity as such begins during this preparation. We ask ourselves: "Now that we have our characters, our settings, our situations, how are we going to tell our story?"

In fact, when the first day of shooting comes I do without the screenplay, not that I'm ignoring it but because I know my story by heart, shot by shot, cue after cue, gesture by gesture. The continuity finished, I begin looking for my cast. I saw sixty people for Mme Arpel, forty for M. Arpel, and so on, even for the small parts.

Inevitably when one does something humorous or with comic pretensions, one is compared to Chaplin. Fifty-seven or fifty-eight films, fifty-six of them successful, it's normal to refer to Chaplin. But they speak without rhyme or reason, they mix styles, and that is very serious. Take the case of a gag which you saw in *Mr. Hulot's Holiday.* He arrives at the cemetery. He needs to get his car started, looks for a crank in the trunk, takes out a tire, the tire is transformed into a wreath, and the funeral director thinks M. Hulot has just brought it. You can say to me: "Hulot didn't find the gag." That's right, he didn't find it. What he did could happen to a man who is scatter-brained, without its having comic invention. Comic invention comes from the screen writer or from the situation, but what happened to Hulot could happen to lots of people. There's a lot of Hulot at bottom, in life. He invented nothing.

In the case of Chaplin, if Chaplin had found the gag good enough to put it in his film—which I'm not sure he would—he would have made the same entrance as Hulot. But, seeing that the situation is catastrophic (his car is disturbing a religious service), on opening the trunk and finding an inner tube, he would himself have stuck the leaves on the inner tube to make a wreath, which would have been accepted in the same way by the funeral director. Thereby the public would have found the character to be marvelous because, at the very moment that no one could have imagined how he could get out of the situation, he invented, on the screen, a gag. And it's the gag that would have set off the laugh, making people say: "He's terrific." One could not say that of Hulot, he was not terrific because that could have happened to you, to everyone; one rummages in a car trunk, something falls out, one picks it up, that's normal. This is where one really sees the two schools, totally different, totally opposite, for Hulot never invents anything.

Buster Keaton doesn't construct, he puts up with. You remember the gag in *The Navigator?* You know, when he hung the portrait of the captain. As the boat pitched one saw through the porthole the face of someone seeming to be watching. It was irresistible.

What's important with Hulot is that he has no concessions. Once the gag is over, one doesn't look farther, one doesn't exploit the formula. Many have reproached me with this. But to take the example I gave at the beginning: that fellow with his tie, his two door curtains and his key, nothing more than that. One could continue to exploit the situation: have his wife arrive and surprise him in the company of a young girl who came to help him, etc. Under the pretext that "that's pictures" one ought to continue, continue. But not at all; what is funny is precisely that it stops there.

I work a great deal on my subject. But I shoot without the screenplay. I know the film by heart and I shoot by heart. I begin at night to go over the theme; I see the images marching along and I memorize them. On the set I know exactly what I'm going to ask of the actors, what I'm going to do; I've no need to go looking for a piece of paper. It's no longer something to be read. And knowing it by heart, I can let myself go, to go all out in my story, without holding back. I don't improvise, I know everything beforehand. The editing too, I do it by the image. I edit the film by heart. Truly, I assure you, in this film I did everything I wanted. If they don't like it, I alone am to blame. I am very concerned to see so many good directors obliged to submit to all sorts of unreasonable demands. Today there are only obligations. Now as for me, I've been able to shoot where I wanted, at Saint Maur, to build the house for Hulot that I wanted. I believe that's important, all the same. There aren't many countries where right now, in film, a fellow can say: I made a film, and I did what I wanted. I adore what Bresson does. Well, it bothers me that he no longer makes pictures.

What's serious, for instance, for the young people is that only one door is opened to them, that of the commercial film. It's very dangerous. After *Jour de Fête*, and especially after *Mr. Hulot's Holiday* I received proposals to shoot a French-Italian co-production. It would have been called *Toto and Tati*. Imagine! I said to myself: "No, Hulot has no right to shoot *Toto and Tati*." Not that Toto is bad—he's a very fine actor. But only because it would be called *Toto and Tati*— that's already dangerous. I think that such artistic independence is obligatory. It's up to us to defend it.

I look to see how people live, I go around, I go to football games, to expositions. I accept some invitations, I stay for hours on the highway to watch the cars go by. I listen to conversations. I observe the tic, the detail, the manner of being that reveals the personality of each individual. I notice that a driver shows himself to be more ill-tempered than a pedestrian because he feels, behind the wheel, caught up in a vast competitive game. I don't look for the message, I'm simply interested in people, families, children, services given, all kinds of little problems that exist in a world more and more blueprinted, mechanized. I would wish that one could "enter" in my next film like one enters a neighborhood both familiar and unknown. I would wish the film to run continuously, that there be tickets at reduced prices so that the spectator could settle down at any hour he wanted, some day when the weather isn't good enough for him to set on the terrace of the corner cafe.

As for me, what I like is observation, and that the comic film becomes satire. Satire about a postman who does his rounds poorly. Satire about vacationers who don't take vacations. But burlesque, it's like the circus. People go there less and less. We're no longer happy enough to go to the circus.

Mime and Something Else
Pinok and Matho

Pinok and Matho (Monique Bertrand and Mathilde Dumont) are two young Frenchwomen who, performing together since 1964, offer a wide range of mime sketches, from comedy to parable, farce to surrealism. They also teach, tour, have authored three textbooks, and occasionally appear as dramatic performers. Their comments were prepared for this anthology.

THE WORD MIME is ambiguous. For many people, mime is make-believe, suggestion, a kind of conjuring (evoking an imaginary object, an imaginary space), and they are right. However, it is something else as well, and it is that "something else" which concerns us. Showing off technique does not. Our ambition is to feel and convey that quivering, that holding back, that vibrating immobility which reveals the secret, inner being, expresses the inexpressible and sees through appearances.

We feel closer to the actor than the dancer, the kind of actor Artaud calls an "emotional athlete" whose whole body—a mass of muscular waves, impulses, contractions and stillness, a perfect transmitter-receiver—could restore that life of the depths, usually invisible, give impetus to its inner impulses and ravages, and embody universal energy in all its forms. The actor who uses bodily gesture evolves in a world like that of the painter and the writer. Painters are not all realists, cubists or impressionists; similarly, the mime actor chooses his style of expression whether it be dreamlike, humorous, fantastic or grotesque. Sometimes people say to us, "That play is dance!" Or else: "You're talking! That's not mime!" If we feel the need to make or use vocal sounds, we do so. If we think props are required, we use them. We want to break down the barrier between the various forms of the art of movement. We do not wish to confine ourselves to one style. We chose mime because, in our opinion, gesture is never ornamental; it is action whereby we are involved, a means for expressing emotions and ideas.

The most important thing for us, while preparing a program, is not finding ideas but pruning and playing down movement ideas out of the flow of material which comes to light during improvisation, in order to try and keep the most important strokes, a picture pared down to the barest essentials. The important thing is to find a body style most suited to the central theme and to the person who wishes to express it.

Figure 23. Pinok and Matho in *Les Reines (The Queens)*. (Courtesy Elisabeth Schweitzer.)

Mime in Great Britain
Clifford Williams

Clifford Williams danced with the Ballet Rambert, with the Markova-Dolin company, and in 1950 formed England's only professional mime company of the time, The Mime Theatre Company. He now devotes his activities to playwriting and directing. This article is taken from Opera, Ballet, Music Hall.

THE STUDENT: I know from my study of theatre history that there have been a number of periods when Mime flourished as an independent and very popular theatre art. But you suggest that Mime may be presented in the contemporary theatre, not merely as a part of some whole—as in ballet or the business of a play—but as something complete in itself. Do you use one of the old mime conventions as a basis for your creations?

THE DIRECTOR: Not at all. Most of these mimetic languages which you allude to—I expect you are thinking of the Roman burlesque mime, the Elizabethan dumbshow, the French pantomime and so on —used languages of gesture in which the gestures formed a visual symbolism of the emotion and thought they portrayed. At their best, these languages represented a genuine stylization based on the movement patterns which were current in those times but often, particularly in passages of descriptive mime, the gestures corresponded to a sort of shorthand which the spectator was obliged to *translate*. Both facets of these languages may appear somewhat arbitrary to our modern audiences which are separated from the manners and customs which influenced these codes of movement by many centuries.

s: Then your repertoire does not contain any mime plays in, for example, the Deburau tradition?

D: In fact, we do perform two Pierrot pantomimes which are very close in mood and technique to his plays. The nearness in time and the comparative simplicity of the gesture used enables the modern audience to accept such plays without difficulties. Moreover, they teach the actor the necessity of informing the most conventional gesture with sincere thought and emotion. But these pantomimes are only a small part of our work: our real task is to discover or forge a mimetic art capable of expressing every subtlety of human behaviour and character.

s: Every subtlety? I believe that Mime has proved an excellent medium for commenting wittily on our foibles and weakness but surely dance is the better technique for the exposition of tragedy.

D: I am glad you have mentioned dance. It is not easy to separate these two arts, but I have always felt—as spectator and executant—that dance is not the most suitable form of movement for the presentation of that dramatic tragedy which arises out of the conflicts between one character and another or character and situation. The psychology of gesture requires minute delineation on occasion—the movement of the eyes alone or the play of facial muscle, and I think that the mime actor is better fitted for this than the dancer who is not concerned with characterization in the same detail as the actor is.

S: You say—*actor!*

D: I assure you that I still consider myself an actor even though I no longer use my voice on the stage.

Mime is not a better but a different theatre art. Where a playwright may take three acts to expose the affectations of his comic hero, the mime artist may well rout such a subject in a few well chosen gestures for our method lends itself to economy and compression. This becomes even more obvious with a tragic situation. In a speech play of the naturalistic genre, a moment of tragedy may well find the hero inarticulate, rooted in silence. The audience may share this moment while it lasts, although the actor is bound—by the convention of his style—to linger no longer than is consistent with the truthful portrayal of a lifelike situation. The mime artist, however, is untrammeled by a naturalistic time and place context. He may, for instance, choose to prolong the tragic moment whilst he probes beneath its surface to discover the innermost impulses which precipitate his character's crisis. He gives rhythmic expression to this in mime which grows purer and more stylised as the innermost recesses of the spirit are penetrated. The audience watches the smallest gesture as in a dream; the rise and fall of the actor's chest attains a new significance; the audience breathes with him—enters the moment—bare and wordless as it is.

Russian Clown
Oleg Popov

One of the most famous clowns in the world, Oleg Popov came to play in the circus from the famed Moscow Circus School. He plays a character clown, performs on the tightrope and slack wire, and plays comic scenes and pantomimes. These excerpts are taken from Russian Clown.

I HAD A SPECIAL fondness for the clowns. When I think back, now, to that period of my life, I am sure that for me they took pride of place among all the other circus acts. In the cinema I idolized Charlie Chaplin. At home I mimicked Patachon, that old-time circus performer, or else I copied Charlie's jerky gait. But not for one moment did the thought cross my mind that the circus might ever become part of my life.

Alley oop! Here I am, the sweeper in Karan d'Ach's sketch "The Statue." I assist him as his comic sparring partner in his interlude "Plates, Bottles" and in other sketches.

Karan d'Ach took an interest in me. In between rehearsals and performances he taught me tricks of the trade which only he knew. Little by little I began to understand the inner essence of a clown's art, things of which no one had breathed a word at the school. I got my second schooling from Karan d'Ach and began to grasp the essential difference between burlesque and the most realistic performance of the clown, to take in the structure of the sequences, of the tricks, of the exits and entrances of a performer. I was deeply conscious that I was learning from Karan d'Ach, that disciple of the famous clowns Vitali Lazarenko and Anatoli Dourov, the ancient art of farce. The legendary names of Karan d'Ach's predecessors filled me with fresh enthusiasm.

I began, little by little, to rid myself of the age-old accoutrements of a clown: the exaggerated make-up, the ridiculous costume. The very simple character I created, a young, unassuming chap, harmonized well with the other acts in the programme. All the performers seemed to have agreed to depict a young man of our times, romantic and full of healthy aspirations, an embodiment of skill, strength, daring and spirit. It fell to me to interpret this last quality. Here is what a Khabarovsk newspaper wrote about the character I portrayed: A modest young man comes out into the ring.

> He wears a simple cap and an ordinary suit. He smiles at the audience as if they are old friends and bows to them. His words

162

have, perhaps, nothing special about them, but the curt, expressive gestures which accompany them bring forth laughter and applause. He is the young clown, Oleg Popov. He has quickly won the sympathy of the audience by the simplicity of his act, the brilliance of his mimicry and the way in which his parodies contrast the other performers' numbers.

At this time my greatest success was a turn called "The Orator." By using mime, without uttering a single word, I created a caricature of a positive windbag of an orator. The speaker "talked" at length, got excited, took off his jacket, his shoes, drank water from a large bucket and wiped his mouth with a blotter. When the audience laughed, I rang a hand bell and called them to order without abandoning my part.

The sketch "The Musical Whistle" was also not without interest. It started with me listening to the musical clowns during their number. Towards the end, I became so carried away by their work that I set about trying to make music myself. I played all kinds of instruments: trumpets, pipes, whistles. I acted the part of a shepherd, a man of the world, a practical joker and, finally, a scolded schoolboy. All these necessarily demanded a complete and swift change of "character."

Little by little I became aware that the success of any character I created depended strictly upon the manner in which I chose to play the part. I always appeared in the guise of a simple, happy chap, perhaps a bit soft-hearted and lyrical. In doing so, I always sought to make my character sympathetic to the audience and in this I succeeded. The make-up, of course, but also the costume, the shoes, the hat, had to take an active part in the creation of the character. Like a vulgar man of fashion I changed coats, shoes and hat, invented different combinations of styles, forms and colours. It was essential that my clothes be extremely plain while, at the same time, remaining expressive.

In search of the best expression for my character's mask, little by little I gave up the too garish make-up—in fact everything which hid, be it only to a small extent, the ordinary human features. All this could not go unnoticed. There were those who considered that I did not have the right to give up the gaudy make-up, the comic disfiguration of my natural features or the exaggerated clothes. "Without them you won't be a clown any more," they told me, "and the circus will stop being what it is." These views were not without good justification. An important part of the clown's act, considering that his exclusive aim was laughter, was to seek to achieve that aim by every means from vivid red wigs down to size 53 boots. This burlesque style as it was called was absolutely unacceptable to me. My ways of expressing myself were already completely different!

The language of pantomime is sometimes more eloquent than everyday speech. I had understood from my first appearance that to a foreign audience my performance would be clearer if there was no need for an interpreter. This would only be possible if I made use of the international language of pantomime. When I prepare a new repertoire I try to enliven it with mimed action. I gave up pure comedy, comedy for the sake of comedy. My object is to get inside the skin of a complete character of an ordinary man and to combine, organically, eccentricity with realism.

In 1953 the producer Youri Ozetov embarked on a trip round all the circuses in the country in order to choose actors for his film *The Ring of the Brave*. I was chosen and came to Moscow. While on the set in the Mosfilm Studios, in front of the cameras, I felt the need to emphasize the expressiveness of my outward appearance. Not satisfied with my first attempt, I shouted out: "Just a moment, please," and dashed into the studio wardrobe. Just inside the door, among dozens of military peaked caps—the "boudionovka" dating from the civil war, and dozens of straw boaters dating from the time of Tsar Nicolas —I found a broad black and white cap checked like a chess board. Most audiences know it now, but it was the film *Ring of the Brave* which made it famous and caused it to become an integral part of my circus costume. Since then it has been part of all my performances, not just passively, but actively as well, for example as a chess board, as the distinctive sign of a taxi and, lastly, as a boomerang which I tried to give a trajectory as precise as that of a sputnik. When Anelle Sudakevich, the circus designer, saw the cap she made me a black suit to go with it. It was an ordinary looking suit, a bit like a Russian caftan. It had nothing eccentric about it except perhaps a certain shapelessness which did nothing except underline the simplicity of my clothing. Black suit, black and white checked cap (which marked the transition to my straw-coloured head of hair), white shirt and neck ribbon: such was henceforward my working outfit. When the clothes had been chosen, my character thus acquired his final appearance.

When I saw myself for the first time in this get-up, which looked so little like the classical ginger-haired comic, funny or terrible, I do not know which, made up like an eccentric and an imposter, I involuntarily asked myself: "But what am I supposed to be?" In order to answer that question it was at once necessary to clarify another: "What is a clown?'' I was to penetrate this mystery eventually, thanks to the great possibilities which offered themselves to me beyond the traditional limits and confines of the clown's act. All this worried me and filled my thoughts at that time but I did not yet know the answer. I was still too young and only my work, my love for my profession, helped by my intuition and the advice of my elders, could give me enough experience to reply to the fundamental question and grasp the significance of what I was doing. A long and difficult path was to lead me there.

A good sketch is like a man; it is born, it grows up and it dies a natural death.

Everything can be used in the ring. But to find the right way, appropriate for the circus, that is the difficult task facing the circus clown.

Movement Theatre
Henryk Tomaszewski

*Henryk Tomaszewski's background is in traditional drama and
ballet; he founded his Wroclaw Pantomime Theatre in 1955.
Comments excerpted from* Tomaszewski's Mime Theatre.

MOVEMENT IS AN affirmation of life. I take it as life, so it is a reflection
of my own life, too. It broadens my own existence, gives it a more
general sense, reduces it to its elements and, at the same time, sums
it up. This is why I attach such great importance to movement and
why I try to construct my theatre through movement. Our mime
theatre proposes to present realistic content using illusionistic means.
Our themes come from literature and from life. It is from them that
we try to draw humanistic inspiration.

Everything in pantomime begins with the *current*. What is meant
by current? The current is our anatomical and mental disposition
which forces the body to perform a definite action. It is something
like an inward order: Begin! Thus the current is a kind of physical
and spiritual mobilization which finds expression in the concentration and readiness of both body and mind. Physical readiness manifests itself, among other things, by the tension of muscles in the area
of the solar plexus, although the tensing of muscles alone is still not
the current.

The current is preceded by a state of complete neutrality on the part
of the mime, expressed by *nothing*. Thus one begins from nothing,
from "zero volume," from barrenness. From this must originate the
mime's self-definition: "I am." I am and I find myself in the central
point of the universe. Everything surrounds me like a cosmic sphere
of which I, the mime, am the centre. Beginning with the Self enables
the actor to pass to the next stage: mobilization upon the order "Here
I start!" The start may be directed against the world or take place in
the face of the world. This happens, for example, in the case of seizing
something, of approaching an object or a person—whenever the
mime's initiative is directed outside. The artist must then achieve
outward current.

When action is to be drawn towards oneself (attraction), from the
world to the mime, it is preceded by inward current. Thus, the deci-
sive thing is the direction of one's state of readiness: towards or away
from the self. Current is a state of mental and physical readiness; the
set and the disposition of the muscles in the area of the solar plexus

are merely one of its visual manifestations, not its essence. The essence, as has already been said, is of a dual nature: both mental and physical. Current is basically that which organizes the mime's movements and maintains him in a state of tension.

The ideal mime is a "sensitive athlete."

My concept of theatre derives, as I have already mentioned, from my concept of the function of movement, its emotional significance, its individualization which determines a given character, etc. Most directors in the dramatic theatre organize the movement of persons on stage and even the movement of the entire production by taking as their point of departure an analysis of the text of the play, a psychological analysis of the part. I proceed the other way round. From the analysis of the movement which the actor has to make in a given situation, I pass to the text. This means that the beginning is movement.

In the theatre, I am interested in works which lead to extreme situations or run into infinity, without a distinct end. This is perhaps why the theatre I crave for, is a 'circular' or, more precisely, a 'spherical' theatre. I call it 'spherical' because the movement which is the essence of my theatre takes place in three dimensions and in time, and therefore requires three-dimensional space, too. Man is the focal point of the 'spherical theatre' and everything takes place around him, at different levels. The theatre thus surrounds him and he should feel the movement even though he does not perform it himself.

Movement is an affirmation of life. I would like somehow to lay man bare before the audience, to show his intimacy, the movement in which man lives for himself and is himself. The function of the theatre cannot be reduced to offering answers to questions and solving people's doubts. Art justifies itself by the mere fact of its existence. It needs no other supports or arguments.

The Art of Dario Fo

Dario Fo

Dario Fo is an Italian actor, director, playwright, mime, dancer, and clown. He writes and plays in films, designs his costumes, sets, and publicity. Fo and his wife Franca Rame devote their efforts to revolutionary theatre through their collective The Commune, *using masks, puppets, clowns, mime, songs, dance, and acrobats. Excerpted from* Mistero Buffo.

ON THE BANKS OF THE Lac Majeur [Fo's birthplace] there were still four or five "storytellers" at the cafe, to whom I listened when I had nothing to do in the evening. They recounted strange stories, a bit artless, a bit mad. Simplicity was their essential characteristic. The stories they told were simple exaggerations based on observation of daily life, but beneath those "absurd" stories was hidden their bitterness; the bitterness of disappointment, and caustic satire on the official world. They related, always in the first person and with an incredible seriousness, the story of strange fishermen who threw their nets with too much force, gathering in the steeples on the other side of the lake, of weird races of barges where the boatman, forgetting to lift anchor, trailed behind him the whole island and obviously came in second; of people who raced snails, and when the snail bumped into a stone, the owners took pity on them and nobly would forego eating them; of strange underwater explorations where one discovered a world like that above water, but still, quite clean, and with, among other things, a beautiful woman with a bow in hand (Diana). When the visitor approached in order to caress Diana, Mercury frowned and stirred menacingly, trying immediately however to resume an attitude so as not to be surprised in that position, for statues are statues and ought always to appear immobile, of course. But either the head turned, or eyes threatened, or the arm stretched forth. I thought the storyteller had invented the stories but I discovered that on the contrary they were traditional. It all stayed within me like a foundation stone.

I learned much from Strehler.* It was a stroke of luck for me to have been able to see him work. I was not part of the troupe, so often I would go up into the balcony, to follow the directing from beginning to end. [But] to write truly political text, one must know firsthand the struggles one talks about; one must go into the occupied

---

*Giorgio Strehler, director at the Piccolo Theatre of Milan.—ED.

factories to discuss their problems with the comrades. Piscator was a great theatre man because he understood that one must make theatre beginning with what touches us most.

Nothing extraordinary in our first revue. There was a pantomime sketch, danced and mimed, about the situation of the Blacks, with blues, that lasted twenty minutes. It needed fantastic breath capacity, for we ran, we jumped, we did the lot. About the Blacks, it was above all a denunciation of the fact that while they were foremost in every way, in sport, intelligence, and so on, they are always relegated to second place. Racism in America twenty-three years ago. How could that message arrive at this point? By means of a cultural current that went through Vittorini, the movements of the avant-garde in Central Europe, Brecht, and so forth. We were politically active people. Caldwell, Camus, Beckett, Sartre. We came out of the ignorance of fascism. We knew nothing. And then we began to read Marx, Lenin, Engels. I tell you, I didn't sleep nights. And then we talked. Each one transmitted to the others an effervescence, a restlessness, even an anxiety.

There are two techniques. One is that of the school of Stanislavski who tells the actor: "You have to dress up in your character to where you enter into symbiosis with it, and you should almost suffer when you take it off after the play"; the other says: "No, when you talk you should speak in the third person. Like someone who succeeds in carrying a marionette as big as himself, and another, on the contrary, who slips inside." We have exploded both of these. In the footsteps of an international school (the French, the Japanese) we have introduced the gesture; no longer "gestire" but as "gestuare," two things very different. "Gestire" means to make gestures; "gestuare" means to construct one's gestures within. Each movement, each step gives meaning. So that if I enter on stage on the diagonal, my speech should be understood in a certain way; if I enter facing, lines assume a different significance.

What was the effect? The precision of the work. People said "like a clock." Nothing left to chance. Even when one played improvising a scenario (because we amused ourselves, we joked, they were lively spectacles, not dead ones) one did variations on the theme. Like the jam session, which is a mathematical, incredible precision.

And that has a deeply political sense. There is, in fact, the problem of a transposition between what is an individualist position and a collective position.

I wanted to go further than a theatre of situations. Instead of creating characters who were fundamentally mannequins, in the tone and rhythm of the avant-garde theatres, in the sense in which one understands avant-garde today; after having disgested avant-garde, expressionism, etc.—it was necessary to go further. And to go further it was necessary to tie up more with the basic popular tradition that still exists in our reactions. Not in making a flat copy, naturally.

I decided to become an artist at the service of the proletarian revolutionary movement, a juggler of the people amid the people, in their neighborhoods, in the occupied factories, in the public squares, the markets, the schools, and to break with institutionalized theatre, not to reform the bourgeois State but to encourage the growth of a revolutionary process susceptible of carrying the working class to power. I directed and played in "Grand Pantomime With Banners and Small and Medium Sized Puppets," on the class struggle between the "dragon" of the proletariat and the "puppet" of the bourgeoisie, using masks, puppets, and marionnettes.

The Fools, or a Strange Dream of a Clown

Ladislav Fialka

Ballet-pantomime characterizes the mime productions of Ladislav Fialka and his Theatre on the Balustrade in Prague. Organized in 1958, the group aimed to create a modern Czech pantomime. Because their explorations were isolated from the French influences of Decroux and Barrault, they drew on ballet, modern dance, and the Deburau traditions of pantomime to evolve their mimodramas. This article is a program note.

Fools had ne'er less grace in a year,
For wise men are grown floppish,
And know not how their wits to wear,
Their manners are so apish.

Shakespeare (*King Lear*, act 1, scene 4)

THIS PANTOMIME—if we are allowed to so call our performance—I never wrote. There is neither a script nor a scenario. The play simply originated and the responsibility thereof is mine. I started with his work more than two years ago. The cast itself did not apprehend, even as late as a year ago, that it was already working on a virtually new *mise-en-scène*. I myself did not know for a long time which definite form the work would take, nor its title. These matters did not even interest me at that stage. All I knew was that everything I wanted to convey must take a form simultaneously consistent and loose, leading to an inspired and precise expression and shape. For a long time I reflected on the pregnancy and wealth of phantasy abiding in the old tragedy and the new clownery. The internal structure of both is close to my heart: they are confined in an almost wonderful way around their central problem, enveloping it as the pulp of a fruit does its stone, but without hiding it. Rather, its existence somewhere in the center of this vivid, succulent and transient substance is stressed by the shape, flavor, and smell of these forms of acting. They do not expose the stone, they do not strip it bare, they do not analyze it; they are only offering themselves whole, stone and all. If we get in touch with the central problem, we may spit it out or we may break its strong hard shell, in order to taste its bitter flavor and smell.

The dramatic, epic, and poetic aspects of tragedy and the kicks, slaps, and gags of clownery may be compared to an always palatable,

171

Figure 24. Ladislav Fialka and The Theatre on the Balustrade in ''The Case of Mr. K'' from *The Fools.* (Courtesy Dana Pasekova and Jaroslav Krejci.)

but more or less appetizing fruit pulp. We enjoy this pulp without thinking about the stone which will finally remain. Nevertheless, we are always striking against this stone and nothing else remains for us to do but to throw the stone away, or try to break its shell. Perhaps it is not necessary to always taste the interior of the stone, for we have already done so on so many occasions in our life. If we have not, we are sure to taste it at least once. Its taste is always the same.

Perhaps because I have known all this before, I have not been particularly concerned with the stone; it simply exists and remains essentially unchanged. I therefore have directed my whole attention to the progressive movement and growth of shape, to the beautiful and exhausting thematic play of myths and tales, to movements and gestures, oscillations and still moments, to the time, colors and tunes, to the space which I anticipated behind every action and creature which began to surround me. I tried to grasp the secret hidden in the difference of similar, and in the similarity of different things. There is a certain unity, an all-embracing, connecting rhythm concealed inside of them.

This work required patience and took a long time. It commanded me to forget much of what I had done and learned so far. When I began, I was travelling with my troupe around the globe and doing a lot of other work, which I liked and which tired me. Finally I began to anticipate the shape that had developed meanwhile around the stone, which forced me to concentrated work. Hundreds of hours of our rehearsals, improvisions, rhythmical and special studies, practice in playing brass instruments, histrionic and acrobatic training—all suddenly acquired their sense. Together with my collaborators, I began to shape the performance. All the Adams, Eves, Clowns, Cains, Eurydices, Hamlets and Ophelias patiently performed their somersaults, played Orpheus's song on their flutes, and beat their drums, repeating a hundred times the same rhythm and motion, often merely with the purpose of purposelessness. We felt sometimes like people doing something void of any logical sense, but all of us knew that in this something lies the sense of everything. We felt like fools. I gave this title to the performance. We searched for a form suitable for all this, we tried to be disciplined and stern, we looked for the courage to eventually be even tedious. We learned this courage from the old myths and from the case of Mr. K.; the determination from Prince Hamlet; the cruel wisdom of the somersault Truth performs out of exuberance, without knowing when and where it will fall down, from fools and buffoons. After a year of work we finally shaped the performance which you may—if you wish—call a pantomime.

For ourselves this work ensues from a desire to detect, in cooperation with the public, the compositional core of these tales we have shaped to only one of their many possible forms. This revelation, achieved by a dialogue between the stage and the auditorium, is the quintessence of the theatre toward which we strive.

The means by which we shall jointly try to come to this recognition is the form, the artistic shaping of the theatre. We are at the scene for reasons identical with those bringing you to the auditorium. Jouvet expressed this in a plain and concise way: ''Forced to comprehend the secret of his life, Man has invented the theatre.''

> When we are born, we cry that we are come
> To this great stage of fools.
>
> Shakespeare (*King Lear*, act 4, scene six)

Figure 25. Ctibor Turba in *Turba Tacet.* (This and the following three photos courtesy Ctibor Turba.)

Figure 26. Ctibor Turba and partner in *Harakiri.*

A Topsy-Turba World

Kuster Beaton

Czech Ctibor Turba exploded on the mime horizon, first with the Alfred Jarry Pantomime Company in 1966, then in his solo surrealist performances from 1970, in conjunction with author and director Jan Kratochvil. Mime, clown, artist, and puppeteer, he performed at his Circus Alfred in Prague, and on tour. He now devotes himself to writing and directing. In this piece Mr. Beaton comments on photographs of Ctibor Turba.

SURE, I'VE SEEN Ctibor Turba. I caught his act after somebody told me he's got my picture on the wall of his set, and sure enough it was there—a big poster. Guess he feels like we're sort of doing the same thing. And he's right.

For instance, there's that piece, "Suicide as a Fine Art," where he's going to commit suicide by electrocuting himself, so he sets up this elaborate Rube Goldberg thing where lots of objects are all connected to each other; finally he sits down between two flatirons that are supposed to clamp his head and transmit the electricity. Well, that reminds me of my sequence in *The Navigator* when the girl and I, who never learned even to boil an egg, as they say, are marooned on a fancy steamship. In the galley are cooking implements for feeding hundreds of people. So I rigged up a complicated device of pulleys and weights and lifts and all, to boil one egg in this huge vat.

Another thing I noticed, we both keep our faces very still, we hardly use any facial expression at all. That puts all the attention on the sight gag and on what we're doing. Because an audience should be able to know what you're thinking just by what you're doing. Once I read something by a professor who said that in this way I made the audience figure it out, participate in the process. I guess so, they seemed to like it.

Seems to me too that Turba and I both concentrate on objects, but in opposite ways. I figure out the logic: a sundial from Roman times tells time, so it seems appropriate to wear a little one on my wrist. Of course the audience knows it won't work. Now when Turba uses objects they're often *not* the appropriate thing; in "Take Him From the Left," when he's getting up and dressed, he uses nonsensical props—puts shoes under the feet of a chair, uses a notebook for a mirror, and so on. And the audience knows that doesn't work either. You could say that I mainly concentrate on the function of things, and he concentrates on the nonfunction of things, and we both end up in the same place. Although, come to think of it, sometimes I did the other too; I once used a broom for a guitar to serenade the girl in *Neighbors*. So maybe we're more alike in that way too.

Also, for both of us, all those objects are important. In his Circus Alfred, Turba is surrounded by objects everywhere—boxes and bubbles and ladders and papers and hats and balloons and musical instruments and furniture and everything you can think of. It reminds me of all those props I had in *The Navigator*, and the way I set up regular housekeeping in *The Boat*, which was like settling down to live on the handcar in *The Railroader*—I always used a lot of props. The difference is that Turba's things are all chaotic and he ends up in a shambles. But me, I have to bring order out of all that chaos, so by the end I have everything neatly under control. Maybe not logical, but under control.

So I guess I'd say that if I was making films now, I'd be playing the kind of ideas that Ctibor Turba puts on stage.

Figure 27. Turba in *The Three Crows Pub.*

Figure 28. Turba in *Turba Tacet.*

Dimitri, Clown
Dimitri

Dimitri, Swiss clown, sports an imposing array of technical skills to support his extraordinary talent. He is a clown-musician, clown-acrobat, clown-juggler. He began performing in the company of Marcel Marceau, then developed his solo productions which he tours world-wide. Dimitri, who is also an artist and ceramicist, runs his own school in Switzerland. In 1973 he received the Grock Prize for his "blending of the surrealist art of the mime with the comedy of the clown." These excerpts come from Dimitri Album.

INDEED, I HAD ALWAYS wanted to be a clown, even as a small boy. But my parents, and I too, thought that a skill would be a good foundation; I apprenticed to a potter. I don't regret it, for I learned a great deal by that profession, and I could practice it again at any time. Certainly it is difficult to play a clown on stage; when one thinks of clown, one instinctively imagines him in a circus. It's by pure chance that I was in Switzerland, that I was associated with the Circus Knie, that I could realize my dream of clown playing in a circus.

Until one finds, in a certain measure, one's personal mask, the mask that sticks to the personality or that corresponds to one's face, that's a story in itself. It's already fourteen years since I've done my solo program, and that time I already had that mask. I didn't invent the white mask, which is classic; I adapted it to myself, and one can see by later photos that the marks under the eyes became longer with the years. Is it by chance that I became sadder? No, certainly not; on the contrary, I feel that I resemble the face of which I dream, and I represent myself under the traits of a clown. When I'm made up I have the impression of approaching a little closer to that face, and perhaps of responding a little better to the poetic being dreamed of by the spectator. There isn't the least doubt that I could very well do my number without make-up, but I think that the make-up offers a certain stylization, a certain strangeness.

It's an almost daily and even nightly confrontation with the complete personage which is the *clown*. When I awaken in the morning my first thought is reserved for my metier, to the *clown*, to the personality of the clown, to the program of the evening, to my physical shape, to the total concentration on the performance, to the feeling that one can always improve. That becomes a part of the daily preoccupation—that I try to improve myself, please the public, give something artistic, something poetic, that I be myself and express

Figure 29. Dimitri in a clown sketch. (Courtesy Dimitri.)

myself as an artist. Despite everything one should remain modest by remembering that in the final analysis one is a grain of sand in this vast world and that there is always someone greater and better who has gotten closer to the goal.

I used to play short sketches. In the course of a program I would give perhaps eight to ten numbers. Now my program consists of two numbers, each one about forty-five minutes long. I always allow for improvisation and for ideas that come to me during the performance; unexpected situations can also occur in the audience. I have many places in which I address the audience directly; I pick up a handbag from some woman and accuse her of having stolen my ping-pong ball, and each night different scenes result. I get the audience to participate and include it in my program. I look at them often, or I do some mimicry, or I let someone spin my plates.

I met Marceau at Paris through some potter friends. Right away he admitted me to his class, and when he saw he could use me in his company he engaged me. We immediately began to rehearse two mimodramas. For me the Marceau period was certainly the most important one in all my studies, for he had an influence on me as a master, as a person, and as a friend. After some 150 performances the engagement with Marceau was ended. In Paris the clown Maisse had seen me work out in a practice studio, and engaged me as a partner to play the Auguste—exactly on the day that Grock died, by rare chance. For a long time that bothered me but perhaps it led to my happiness. I learned an enormous amount with Maisse; he is a great clown, especially his white clown, partner of Auguste. He had also been partner to Grock.

A number with a comic automobile in which my children performed for the first time as real artists, doing acrobatics and playing musical instruments: We arrive in the arena in the auto; we want to stop and play music and have a good time. Knie junior [ringmaster] wants to send us away, saying that we can't stop there, we'll interfere with the program. We get back in the car, but each time he leaves we get out again, and so on. Finally he says: All right, you can play for just a few minutes, and then you leave immediately. Only when we go to leave, the motor won't start. I get nervous and try to get the car started, and all kinds of things happen until finally the car starts and runs—without us.

In one number I try to catch the light from a spotlight. But I take pity on it and let it escape through a hole in the top of the tent. The idea of a cone of light usually goes like a leitmotif through all my circus appearances.

There isn't the least doubt that a number doesn't mature except in contact with the public; for that reason I don't film them* as soon as they are created. A year later it is always better, for it has been well broken in, refined and polished. I think that a number never stops improving, for I work it constantly. I modify and polish without end, I drop certain sections and add others. When they see it a year later, many spectators assert that it's a different sketch. It's like a child growing up.

---

*Dimitri films his pieces for his records; they contain hundreds of details that are easy to forget. —ED.

Mask, Mime, and Mummenschanz
Mummenschanz

The Mummenschanz are two-thirds Swiss (Andres Bossard and Bernie Schurch) and one-third Italian (Floriana Frassetto). Their unique program consists entirely of masked pieces. Working in their present form since 1972, and touring world-wide, they inspire many other mimes to experiment with masks. The Mummenschanz opened a New York Broadway engagement in March 1977 and established the unheard-of record for a Broadway run of mime, over two years at present writing. These passages appeared in Mime Journal *in an article by Bari Rolfe.*

BERNIE: I was working very much the classical mime, the white mime, and this is also a mask. It fascinated me years before, but the real flip was at Lecoq's studio.

ANDREAS: We said, now we must cut down everything and just look where we are, where is our thing. So we lived about six months in total isolation. We were out of the country, we didn't hear the radio, no newspapers—some books perhaps—no cinema, no television, nothing. Absolutely on our own. And that was the moment, the initial moment when we suddenly felt things coming out of us which were absolutely our own, not influenced by anything or anybody. Because very often I think a young artist makes a big mistake. He doesn't know exactly what to do, he's searching and he's imitating others. It's a kind of courage to drop everything, not to go with moods and fashions. . . . First is the information, to know what's going on all around; then he must take a distance and have the courage to be on his own.

It's abstraction, I think it's the law of abstraction in art. You don't think to do it that way; at first it's a very naturalistic work. Then it's cut cut cut till we have the initial pattern coming through. While we are discussing the improvising, we think to make it accessible to the audience by purifying it of all our anecdotal stuff. Then it's a drama which is *our* drama but everybody can fulfill it with his own life, put himself in it. That for me is the definition of art, not just reproduction, but the state of finding—like for example African tribal masks. You never find a mask which is called "gazelle mask "—it is called "ghost of gazelle mask." They would not reproduce the animal, but the state, the ghost of gazelle.

The face, okay, it's the most important feature but it's not absolutely the most truthful. It's very cheating; we can always cheat with

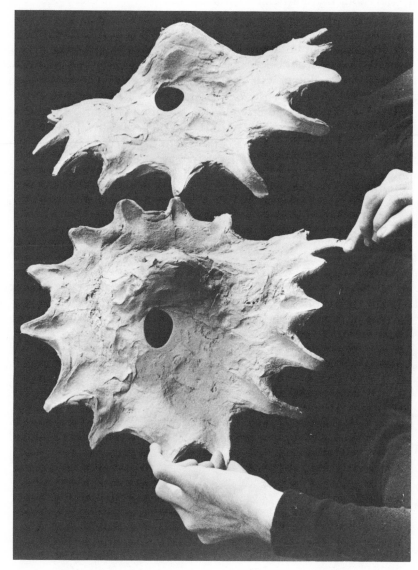

Figure 30. Mummenschanz. (Courtesy Arthur Shafman International, Ltd.)

our faces. But with the body we cannot cheat. So we should look more at bodies when we are meeting people, we would learn more. But speaking is even more of a mask. We can see this in politics. We look at television, the politicians speaking and with just their face. They should stand up speaking. Then it would be awful! They would show us everything! They wouldn't be able to mask any more.

BERNIE: If we could transpose the ability of masking our own face into the body it would be perfect. I mean for acting. If we can just transpose, push down into the body what we use of our face and talking.

ANDRES: There are people who see our show and are impulsively thinking "Wow! I would like to make masks too!" But there is a very deep thing with masks; I had it in my own experience. When you are an actor you are used to having your face, your body, your ego, to show on stage. So when you go into masks . . . Even in our first show we said, "Okay, masks, but perhaps two or three acts without masks." Slowly we got used to being absolutely covered the whole show through. Sometimes you feel really like an auxiliary, like a puppet, so your ego . . . . But that is wrong, because in time you get another view. You feel even closer to the public, you feel more exposed and showing. But that's not everyone's cup of tea.

Sometimes it's incredible how far away is the effect we produce from what we think we produce with these shapes.

FLORIANA: Actually this started as a study of cubism. We were more or less searching the shapes they could form together. Then the audience started telling us that these were two little heads, or two cars, and they preferred to see them kiss. Very often people see opposite things of what we see and that makes the conversation very interesting.

ANDRES: That act with the cubes, for example, can be for people just a game, or a discussion, or a mental exchange. Some see in it the cruelty of psychiatry because brain cells are taken out and replaced, and others see money, they see possessions.

BERNIE: It's a game of thoughts. The cubes, they represent thoughts.

Zen Mime
Mamako Yoneyama

> *Mamako Yoneyama, Mamako the Mime, is a young Japanese woman who performs in theatre, film, and television, and frequently teaches. Part of her repertory is composed of French-style sketches wittily applied to Japanese life. Recently she developed a special genre which she calls Zen Mime, epitomized in her interpretation of the Zen story "The Ten Bulls." These comments are taken from her program notes and commentary.*

As a JAPANESE, I can't think MIME without thinking about ZEN. The essence of ZEN is to teach yourself how to experience the joy of VOID as it was experienced by Buddha. MIME, as silent art, resembles the way of ZEN.

When we think about HAIKU, it is one of the art forms which is born from ZEN. This creative process seeks the same state of being as MIME does. HAIKU is a poem composed of only three lines. In this brief statement, all of life's phenomena are expressed as inspirationally, as existentially and as economically as possible. These few words are dropped into the pond of silence. They ripple for a moment and then silence returns.

The mutual communication of word and silence. This is HAIKU and this is MIME. I think MIME is *HAIKU in movement.* As movement becomes simpler and simpler it gradually enters into the world of VOID or ZEN which is the same.

What a YUGEN (mysteriously profound) art MIME is!!

The world is growing more polluted with noise and plastic. I love mime as I love clear rivers, quiet forests and deep ponds.

The soul of MIME is this calm nature and it must not be polluted!

*　　　　　*　　　　　*

My forty-minute-long piece, called "The Search for the Bull," was created from the Zen doctrine "The Ten Bulls," using the symbol of man trying to capture and tame the bull. It shows the process of Zen training, the lifelong search for enlightenment.

The bull in these stories means searching for my true form in myself. When I was a youth in Japan, society did not allow the woman to be independent. It was difficult for a woman to realize her own aim in the real life. Also, situations are too confused for an artist to grow favorably. After the war, Japan had suddenly become a victim of mass

185

Figure 31. Mamako in a Western pantomime. (Courtesy Mamako.)

communication. I left Japan and had a journey in the United States. I saw a freedom of a great many new creations and sometimes I saw a freedom of idleness, possessiveness and ruined environment. I had difficulty understanding the frank openness of the people. In Japan desires of the individual are hidden by many customs and words. As a foreigner in the American "wilderness of feeling," a lonely human being is obliged to fight against her own hunger for love, possessiveness, power complex, desire of self-elevation, lust, etc.

America is the perfect place for me to realize my own weakness and frailties. Deep inside a natural life force struggles against the melancholy and it gradually becomes "the angry Bull." So the process, in which the angry Bull gradually turns into an enlightened Bull, is itself hope for psychotherapy/personal growth/for myself and many others.

The sorrow of a woman who searches for enlightenment but keeps failing is revealed in the clownishness of her behavior. "The Ten Bulls" is my life's work. Every year I present a new arrangement as my understanding matures.

How Sweet It Is . . .

Lotte Goslar

Lotte Goslar, after coming to America from Germany in 1939, has offered her comedy mime and comic dance in musicals, theatres, on the concert stage, and on television, in New York and on international tours. Goslar heads her own unusual company of dancer-clowns, The Pantomime Circus. The following article was written for this book.

How sweet it is—success, applause, good reviews—friends coming backstage to tell you you've never been better—strangers saying "Where have you been all my life?" In spite of the fact that you know full well it could not have been all that good, how sweet it is . . .

My biggest success came in Chicago, where I performed with the great actors George Voskovic and Jan Werich (refugees like myself) in a special program for their Czechoslovakian compatriots. I had danced some years before in their fabulous Liberated Theatre in Prague, and now I was in join them again on that special evening, performing some solo pieces. I had just finished my first number, a short curtain-raiser, when an avalanche of applause broke loose such as I had never experienced before. Not three curtain calls, not five, not ten, but at least fifteen! At that time I always took my bows in character, and pretty soon I was out of fresh ideas. I could not see the audience because the spotlights were shining directly, blindingly, into my eyes. Finally I went as far to the front of the stage as possible to get a look at this extraordinary crowd. And I saw that they all had risen to their feet and were standing with their backs toward me. What had happened: Eduard Benes, the president-in-exile, their great hero, had arrived and was standing in the balcony. The entire out-break of applause had been for him! And I had taken my bows—in character!!!—toward their behinds. The only one who had seen me making a fool of myself was Benes. I hope.

I also remember fondly our premiere in Amsterdam. During a hectic performance three little boys kept coming backstage and pestering us for autographs. Of course we gave them, pretending only a little an-noyance, because after all, even if they were only kids, here was a new generation, our future audience, clamoring for us. Until we dis-covered that the same little boys came back several times, and finally we found out that they were selling our autographs on the street—for five cents!

How far does one go to keep success rolling? Well, in Italy, where an insane manager had publicized us as "Balletto di Hollywood,"

Figure 32. Lotte Goslar in *Grandma Always Danced.* (Courtesy Sheldon Soffer Management, Inc.)

and where as a result the square in front of every theatre was filled with young men waiting for hours to see the glamorous stars arrive, I simply asked one of my beautiful young dancers to step out of the car first as if she were me, and I would follow her carrying suitcases as if I were her dresser. It worked. There was a howl of appreciation for her.

And what about this kind of success? Again, in Holland, we had been on TV and were utterly disgusted with the result. The next morning as I was walking on Calverstraat, a man on the other side of the street called over to me: "I saw you on TV last night. Wow!" "Oh," I said, "I thought it was terrible." "Right!" he said.

To be copied is supposed to be the ultimate praise. In Switzerland a young mime travelled around doing an entire program of my numbers, without mentioning my name. That, I thought, was a bit much and when I met him I told him so. He could not understand my concern. "But Lotte," he said, "I'm a Communist. Your work is needed by the masses. I'm giving them what they need. You are trying to deprive them." He had a point!

My favorite "success" story happened in New York, years ago when things were especially rough for me. No engagements, no manager, no students, no money. Nevertheless, I managed, as always, to live in a place that could serve as a studio, so at least I could dance. The building was old, the elevator rickety, the elevator man a little shriveled guy. On one of the most dismal, cold, rainy days he brought me up to my third floor studio. During the slow, slow ride to the first floor he took a long look at me with his little beady eyes and said: "You know, Miss Gosling, you are not beautiful." That was all I needed on this grey morning. "Alright," I said, "I know." Silence. Between the first and second floors he looked at me again, long and slow. "You aren't even pretty," he said. "Okay," I answered, "rub it in." He opened the door to the third floor for me and as I was trotting down the hallway, cold and dejected, I heard him yell: "But you've got what it takes!" Now that I call success, don't you?

Another memory of that sort, but much more delicate, has to do with a time when I was engaged to perform in a summer show near New York many years ago. It was a mixed program of several New York artists and we all arrived a few days before the first performance. So there was time to get acquainted. Among many others there was a young pianist, Paul Draper's accompanist, who obviously liked me. We went for walks, or he played, beautifully, from his concert repertoire for me. And he would always look at me with shy, warm eyes. Never more. The day of the performance came and I was standing in the wings ready to go on. The number was called "Old Clown" and I had totally disguised myself to portray the character. My body was completely covered with an outrageous potato sack; huge shoes and gloves hid my feet and hands; my hair was under a wig; my nose under a big bulb; and make-up covered every bit of my own skin. There was no me to be seen, but only an old, old, overstuffed Clown. The young man was standing next to me. I felt his warm, shy look on me and this is what he whispered into the huge plastic ear that covered my own: "You are lovely."

Figure 33. Dick Van Dyke in *Darts.* (Courtesy Dick Van Dyke.)

Mime in the Medium
Dick Van Dyke

Dick Van Dyke is best known as a television comedian; he is an actor, mime, comic, and eccentric dancer. He played pantomime in night clubs (The Merry Mutes) before beginning his twenty-eight year television career, and has featured the Los Angeles Mime Company on some of his shows. These comments were prepared for this anthology.

STAN LAUREL'S COMEDY strongly influenced me to go into show business in the first place, and his influence molded my point of view, my attitude about comedy.

I once did an impression of Stan Laurel on my first TV series. I took meticulous care to get everything just right—clothes and all. After the show I called him to ask how it was. He said, "It was fine, Dicky, but . . . " and then he gave me a list of things I'd done wrong—for forty minutes. In that call he said more about show business than I could ever learn.

I like playing physical gags, the sort of thing closer to the silent films of Chaplin, Keaton, Laurel and Hardy—it's my kind of comedy. After all, I was brought up on their films. When I was a youngster, I spent Saturdays, all day, watching their movies.

Today, networks make it hard to be free and original with variety shows; they usually want a standard, safe formula. They think they have to put in something for everybody, what they call demographics. But I don't agree with that philosophy; I know when I look at television, I want to see what I want to see. When I want to enjoy a track meet, I have to get through a demolition derby before I get to the meet. I'm a track nut. That was my thing in high school. I'd love it if I could be a commentator at the Olympics.

When I began in night clubs in a pantomime act called "The Merry Mutes," it was all slapstick, falls, and physical comedy. I was glad to get back to it. We tried to build a good stock company for my show, Van Dyke and Company—a group of people who worked well together, whose gears meshed. But it takes time to evolve such a company, and time is what you don't get these days in this medium. The ratings were low, so Van Dyke and Company was cancelled after only eleven shows.

I enjoy doing the sitcom shows, but they don't give me much room to stress the physical comedy part. Lots of people didn't even know I did pantomime and comedy dance. In the new shows, I wanted particularly to do mime, so I was using the L.A. Mime Company. The shows were highly praised by critics who called them original, fresh, and inventive. And on every test we've done, mime has rated first.

I feel good about doing a good show, whether it's high in the ratings or not. When you're young, the ratings' pressure can drive you up the wall.

But now I worry less, enjoy it more.

American Mime
Paul J. Curtis

The first mime company in the United States, The American Mime Theatre, was founded by Paul J. Curtis in 1952. In his New York school Curtis has developed a rigorous, personal style, containing elements from his background as actor and dancer. Curtis initiated the professional organization, International Mimes and Pantomimists, in 1973. Comments here were prepared for this anthology.

I WANTED TO create a dramatic event that would combine acting and moving to produce a more meaningful theatrical experience. This work slowly produced a different performing art from that of the traditional French pantomime. American Mime is simply a particular balance of the arts of acting, movement, pantomime, design, and playwriting. It is a complete theatre medium in a way that no other mime form I know of is. That means there is a complete body of aesthetic laws and limitations governing every aspect of its activities from performance to script material that insures the consistency of its aesthetic products.

The primary aim of our medium, regarding script material, is to explore the internal landscape. We create mime plays that are made up of activity symbols. These activities must be logical on the narrative level and yet clearly communicate the symbolic significance behind them. Our content is myriad forms and facets of spirituality. It is our aim in performance to elicit from the audience through their intellects and emotions a direct spiritual response. We choose each play out of what individually and collectively concerns us most of the time of creation and in relationship to what we already have in the repertory.

In performance, from five to seven different plays are performed, each of them representing a different aspect of American Mime script material. Our performers appear in black skintight units before a white cyclorama.* Sets are never used. Masks, costumes, properties, and set pieces are used sparingly and are created to be frankly theatrical. We try to produce a lean clean look by using equipment created to suggest more than it shows. We use very little music. Our sound ranges from abstract vocal sounds made by the performers to electronic scores. Once in a great while the play will contain a special use of one word. We don't use white face.

---

*Concave backdrop hung at the rear of a stage. —ED.

Figure 34. Paul Curtis and The American Mime Theatre in *Dreams.* (Courtesy Paul Curtis.)

The American Mime Theatre is known as a "serious attraction," an artistic success. Loosely translated this means our work is generally not as bad as most of the professional theatre, we believe in what we are doing, and have money trouble. Being an American Mime performer in the United States at this time in history is a commitment rather akin to becoming a Trappist monk in Italy in the seventeenth century; the theatre is kept alive not by popularity, or the psychological necessity of its products, but by the internal need, or compulsion, of its practitioners to practice it in order to lead a creative life. We practice this medium as a way of life. We spent the first fifteen years of our life developing our medium. Now we are committed to the evolution of a superior creative product and the promotion of this medium throughout the world.

Commedia and the Actor
Carlo Mazzone-Clementi

> *Carlo Mazzone-Clementi performed in his native Italy, in France,
> and came to the USA in 1957. He has worked with Marcel
> Marceau, Jacques Lecoq, and other well-known artists, as a mime,
> an actor, and in* commedia dell'arte, *where he specialized in the
> role of Brighella, zany servant. His school, The Dell'Arte School
> of Mime and Comedy, was opened in 1971 in California and offers*
> commedia, *mime, and comedy. The following is excerpted from
> an article in* The Drama Review.

ALTHOUGH WE CAN conjecture about *commedia* in a historical framework, we cannot *know* what it was like. There are no existing scripts,
no photos. There are only a few paintings, a few sparse descriptions,
and a horde of mostly untranslated scenarios. Yet, a great interest in
commedia continues. Anyone can open the drawer marked *commedia
dell'arte*, but, having opened it, how does one know what to choose
from it? For some, *commedia* means a dusty reincarnation of the
postures and poses of a Callot, charming in print, but deadly on the
stage. The magnetic appeal of *commedia*, for me, has been to rediscover the magic of the performer; how he worked, what he did, and to
some extent, why he did it, consciously or not. The only possible
approach is an inductive one. We must begin where we are.

How, then, does one approach the study of *commedia* in the twentieth century? My first approach was through the discipline of mime.
Two Frenchmen have had great influence on my work: Marcel Marceau
and Jacques Lecoq. I worked with both when I was young. Through
them—and through a short period as a scholarship student at the
school of Jean-Louis Barrault—I first met mime. I was fortunate enough
to travel around Italy with Marceau, performing with him, responding to his creativity. Philosophically, mystically, and poetically, he
was a catalyst for me. Practically, however, it was Lecoq's excellent
systematized natural method that confirmed my intuition regarding
mime—that it was to be the basis of all my theatrical work, and that
it was to open many doors in my understanding of *commedia*. Both
Marceau and Lecoq were obsessed by *commedia*. Witnessing their
fascination with it, and later, at the Barrault school, coming into contact with more Frenchmen who were *commedia* enthusiasts, I felt for
the first time a sense of my own national and cultural identity.
Through the French, I discovered what it meant to be Italian. In their
pantomime blanche, I saw an extension of *commedia*, the legacy of

Pedrolino (Pierrot) and Scaramouche. As the French theatre once used Italian *commedia* for its source and creative inspiration, so I have drawn on the teaching of Lecoq for my work in *commedia*.

Characterization must begin at home: in the body. Some of us are not at home in our bodies. We must discover what that means. Therefore, the main emphasis of my work is physical self-discovery. In his book, *Reflections on the Theatre*, Jean-Louis Barrault speaks of the actor as constantly going "from—to." "How" is a character. Beginning where you are means *really* knowing where you are, from your heels up, and not (for the moment at least) avoiding contact with reality through flights of the imagination, philosophical excursions into existentialism, or even emotional recall.

The most simple act of going "from—to" is the RUN. That is where we start. Running is a primary physical activity. It circulates the blood, activates the heart, exercises the lungs, and drives extraneous thoughts from the mind. The motion of this act is dominated by the contact of foot and floor—inhaling, exhaling, turning, wheeling, sweating, as you follow the leader. Do you run badly? You will discover it in motion. Is your body unresponsive? Thinking about it will not help. The kinesthetic response comes only with motion. Kinesthetic response is not a product of brute energy. Paradoxically, the difficult must be easy.

We cannot talk of *commedia*, or my approach to it, without discussing both mime and silent movies. Charlie Chaplin, Buster Keaton, Mack Sennett, Harold Lloyd, Harry Langdon, Marie Dressler, W.C. Fields were all able to use any fuel for their creative fires. "You talk first, and I'll talk next" was a scenario. No matter what the material, the true comedian will know how to use it!

Through the ages, everyone has used *commedia* for his own purposes, from Moliere, who openly proclaimed, "I take my best where I can find it," to Shakespeare, Brecht, and the political street theatre groups of our own time. I do not pretend to have rediscovered *commedia* as it was in the Renaissance. In fact, that seems to me a shallow and limiting approach to *commedia*. But a kind of theatre that points out our human frailties and foibles in such an honest, unpretentious way, a theatre in which actors are skillful, perceptive, inventive, united, and generous, seems to me to be much needed today. In a world gone mad, who has more to say to us than the zanies? Well, the Venetians have a proverb, "If they aren't crazy, we don't want them." And *commedia*, after all, is not a theatrical form, it is a way of life.

Price of Folly

Antonin Hodek

Antonin Hodek, Czech mime now living in Los Angeles, is also a writer of children's stories, poet, teacher, and playwright. His clown character August (from the circus figure Auguste) is his recent creation. These remarks are from his program notes.

When I die, my clown
please, lay me down
into a big black derby
under a rubber tree—
And let the Scarecrow, my patched Pierrot
play his blues
his bluest blues
for me.

I AM AFRAID that in our manipulated world of today only the arts are capable of giving us the faith, the hope and the strength to get through. Live theater especially makes the immediacy of warm human relationships possible.

We all live in a foolish world; unless we want to become mad, we have to become fools ourselves,

> . . . because in every good clown we find something of ourselves, something of our most secret and most pure wishes and longings. That is why we laugh at a good clown. But at the same time our heart is full of anguish, and perhaps we shall even cry. In the end we cannot really tell whether we laugh or cry, but most probably we do both at the same time. While looking at a good clown a painter has an urge to paint, a drinker wants to drink, and thieves promise themselves to steal no more, and all of them want to live somehow differently. When a good clown performs, one has a feeling of a special inner purity; it is a pity that the world has so many buffoons and so few clowns . . . (Kludsky)

Once I performed for Los Angeles children. None of them had ever seen pantomime before. The word pantomime was for them just as unknown and exotic as for me, in my childhood, the spice-flavored word, Panama. From black paper the children made a three-yard placard and they glued on it a picture of three multicolored fellows in stripped T-shirts. Above the picture there was a blue text:

PANTOMIME IS A COUNTRY WITH A CANAL IN IT

That, my friends, is a sentence which can be rolled over the tip of your tongue and tasted over and over again.

200

That, my friends, is a vision that gently wakes the imagination in a way we would wake a beautiful girl whom we see for the first time, at dawn, and just as the gods created her—sleeping, smiling and promising.

And in these early silver hours of the morning we usually carelessly pledge ourselves for life. And this is why we have to pay for it—this is the price of folly.

Mime: Self-Imposed Silence

Samuel Avital

Moroccan-born Samuel Avital opened his mime school, Le Centre du Silence, in Colorado in 1971. Avital looks at mime from his special view as a Kabbalist. This piece is excerpted from an article in The Movement.

A FIRST MIME PREPARATION is to come to know the human body through exercise and experience. We offer some practices that help the students on the way to be in the proper frame of mind and to be willing to be taught. In other words, a student must first learn how to learn.

A mime, according to my standard, must transform his way of thinking first, by very elaborated, constant practice. We learn to think words in this culture. A mime must think movement, vision, images and non-linearly; and this process must be given unlimited time to explore. Only when this new way of thinking is mastered can one begin with the analytic work. Later improvisation comes to enlarge the scope of the work. One of our practices is to fast from words one day a week, to bring this to a habit, in order to penetrate the realm of silence. Later, we shape this silence with movement, giving it a multidimensional reality.

Coming to mime from an Eastern way of thinking helps me to see clearly the way of the West. Since my upbringing was spiritually rooted, in what I do or think there is a spiritual awareness. As a performer, a mime, and a teacher, many ways present themselves to me to impart that spiritual awareness to the students that come my way. We would like to reach higher in this art, from better to excellence. The key for this is the awakening of spiritual reality in the student, with no attachment to dogma. It is real when, in the process of becoming, the student discovers the self. Only through disciplined work can one begin to realize his aspect of inner beingness. This development will lead and assist the student to rise above all mediocrity, not only in his art, but also in his life. For me mime is a way of being and becoming. Mime is more than an art, it is a way of life; it requires metaphysical as well as physical awareness. It is an extension of the life force, a channeling of energies into a symphony of being. Mime is not just a skill of acting without words. It is a process of expanding the consciousness beyond mere sensivity, time, and space. It is being able to communicate this expansion clearly, with artistic skill, on the stage, in order to reflect the human condition in our puzzled times.

Bernard Bragg and the
National Theatre of the Deaf

Helen Powers

*Bernard Bragg pursued a mime career for ten years, playing in
cabarets, then in his own television show, "The Quiet Man."
A founding member of the National Theatre of the Deaf, he was
a featured player for another ten years. Bragg has also written and
published poetry. These passages are selected from* Signs of Silence.

BERNARD FELL IN LOVE with the stage at a very early age. From the
movies he saw, he soon learned to do his own imitations of such
Hollywood greats as Charlie Chaplin, Mae West, and Charlie Chan.
He quickly discovered that this was one means by which he could
communicate with the world he couldn't hear.

When Bernard returned to Gallaudet in the fall of 1948 to begin his
freshman year at college, his love for the theatre pushed more and
more into the fore. He took all the courses he could in drama and
majored in English literature. He played the lead roles in *The Miser*,
The Merchant Gentleman, and *Tartuffe.* In his last year he was given
an opportunity to direct John Galsworthy's *Escape.* There was no
question in Bernard's mind, or anyone else's, but that he belonged on
the stage.

Bernard sat high in the theater to see the legendary Marceau, so he
could observe the audience's reaction to an evening of silent movement. The house lights went out, and one spotlight illuminated a
circle on the dark velvet curtain. After a suspenseful moment, the curtain went up, and Marcel Marceau occupied the stage. Bernard was
enthralled. He became even more excited as he watched the audience's
response to this man who kept them entertained by mere motion,
and no sound. This was the language of silence, the communication
that needed no words. He had to talk to Marceau.

Bernard performed as a pantomimist wearing the traditional white-
paint mask and costume. Thus attired, his own identity was subli-
mated by that of the "universal man." He wanted to reach his audiences as the central symbol of their own lives, without personal dis-
traction. When he was confident that his acting had achieved this
level of universality, he discarded the mask and costume and relied
solely on his performance to sustain the penetrating significance of
his act.

Figure 35. Bernard Bragg, June Russi, William Rhys, in *The Critic.* (Courtesy Helen Powers.)

He had a wide repertoire in his one-man show. He was totally involved in each performance, and had no problem casting himself in a multiplicity of roles. One of these was an episode involving the first space traveler to the moon, who proceeds to claim it for America by raising the Stars and Stripes on its sandy soil, only to discover that the Russians got there first. This, of course, was extremely timely in 1958. The broad range of his self-invention included humorous portrayals of "Psychiatrist and Patient," "Jealous Wives—French, English, Italian, and American," and "Shoplifter in a Sporting Goods Store." The highlight of his show, however, and an innovation in the world of mime, was the impromptu portion, during which he took suggestions from the audience and interpreted them on the spot.

A mime must be, first and foremost, a student of life. Bernard's opportunity to observe people he could not hear put him at the head of the class. Whether he was riding a bus or queued up for theater tickets, he was acutely aware of facial expressions and gestures. These he could then summarize with his own artistic economy. His qualities emerged not in spite of his deafness but because of it.

The National Theatre of the Deaf had its inspirational beginnings when a group of performers from Gallaudent College presented their production of *Iphigenia in Aulis* at Eugene O'Neill Memorial Theatre in Waterford, Conn. The first formal meeting of NTD culminated in the NBC Special which was taped in March 1967. The NTD has turned sign language into a ballet of hands to lend visual appeal to the stage, thus giving words an added dimension. This theatricalized version of sign language virtually eliminates finger spelling, as words or concepts are "mimed" with the hands. The sign-mime adaptation for the theater is thought-for-thought to capture a word-for-word translation. Nuances, shadings, and modifications are brought into play by the manner in which the word is signed, together with the accompanying facial expression and body movement. On stage, or off, it is a physical language as flexible as an oral one when properly employed and artistically mastered. It was one of the purposes of the theater to show the logical beauty of the language of signs to its audiences, and to alleviate misconception and misjudgment of those whose lives are attended by silence.

It didn't take long before the viewer no longer saw "signing" as such, but, rather, graceful finger interpretations that enhanced the actions and the voices, hands that spoke and bodies whose rhythm accentuated the meaning. One lost all awareness of "deafness" and basked solely in the pleasures of a new and dynamic art form. In order to maintain the purity of the script and clarify communication, "narrators" simultaneously speak the lines with the actors as the signing takes place. The exact timing between the deliveries is so precise that the hearing viewer is no longer conscious of the "readers." This supplementary vocal assist at no time overshadows the powerful emotional impact of the actors themselves.

Time at Waterford was evenly divided between body movement and acting. New York director Jack Sydow instructed in acting. His classes were conducted in the same manner as acting classes for the hearing would be, concentrating on emotional involvement and instinctive blocking. It is incumbent upon the deaf performer to keep his hands visible at all times to his audience, and to other members of the cast. He cannot "speak" a line with his back turned, as his hearing counterpart might do. Class work consisted of lectures, and group participation in scenes from various plays which were then open to comment, criticism, and direction.

Closely allied to the acting classes were those in sign-mime, conducted by Bernard and Eric Malzkuhn. More expressive than words, sign-mime gives sound a visual dimension never before achieved. It also eliminates the necessity of finger spelling, as this is difficult for the deaf audience to see or read in a theatre. A new descriptive sign is created for words that might be spelled under sitting-room circumstances. As the deaf actor's hands are comparable to the hearing actor's voice, coaching is conducted on that premise. As the stage voice must be raised to sound normal in the theater, so the manual movement must be exaggerated to look normal.

Creativity is another aspect of the sign-mime lessons. The students must adapt sign language to words as they perform scenes in class. Finger spelling is discouraged and replaced by new signs created to by-pass the tedium of spelling words for which no sign exists. All of this, of course, must be done within the bounds of sign languages so that the meaning will not become obscure to the deaf person who sees it.

Method in Mime
R. G. Davis

> Ron Davis came to California and opened what he announced as
> "San Francisco's Oldest Mime School" in 1959. His San Francisco
> Mime Troupe, established 1962, pioneered the mobile, set-up
> performances in the parks, playing commedia dell'arte and contro-
> versial, agit-prop material. Davis is the author of San Francisco
> Mime Troupe: The First Ten Years. These comments were prepared
> for this anthology.

SINCE THE thirties, the Stanislavski system has been the dominant
approach to acting for the greater part of the literate theatre. The
Method found support from American psychiatry, which influenced
actors' technique by focusing attention on emotional content, "real
responses," and high dramatic sincerity. In emphasizing the dramatic
or psychological elements of the performance, visual imagery, movement and design were overpowered by tears, sweat, grunts and honest
emotions. There were, of course, numerous disputes, but the context
of the disputes was Stanislavski's analysis of how to resuscitate emotions and create imaginatively on stage. In theory, Stanislavski's
system (internal motivation) extends to all aspects of performance.
Yet efforts to effect a synthesis of movement and Method have proved
troublesome. Modern dance has decidedly left its imprint on the
musical theatre, but aside from reawakening the actor to movement,
it has not deepened his craft. The approaches of dancer and actor to
the problems of performance appear in most cases incompatible. So
too with pantomime. Marcel Marceau brought pantomime to this
continent's attention. It looked like excellent "sense memory," a
closing of the gap between movement and the actor. But investigation
revealed its technique; pantomime, too, was external.

"Method in Movement" simply means motivating external movement from an internal source. The end product is neither modern
dance, nor any of its variants, nor pantomime and its pictures. In
the main, modern dance and mime are relatively distinct from one
another. While mime and pantomime have been used interchange-
ably to describe anything from white face acts to improvisational
performances without props, the distinction between mime and pantomime is not merely academic; rather, one form is compatible with
a Stanislavski acting technique, and advances from that kind of analysis, while the other is not.

In *Medieval French Drama*, Grace Frank distinguishes between the
heritage of mime and pantomime: " 'Mimus' covered performances of

diverse forms ranging from extemporaneous fooling of the lightest sort to more serious types of comedy that might, at least in part, be committed to writing. 'Pantomime' consisted essentially of solo dances performed to the accompaniment of singing and musical instruments . . ." Going back still further in time, Allardyce Nicoll notes in *Masks, Mimes and Miracles*, "The Doric Mimes gave us a non-choral drama where farcical plays introduced grotesquely clad stock figures, most of them wearing the phallus, who represented scenes of real life alongside mythological burlesque. In all probability, most of the dialogue was improvised." The work of two performers illustrates the difference as it exists in contemporary culture. Marcel Marceau is basically a Pantomimist. Charlie Chaplin is a Mime.

Marceau deals with "nothing there,"—it is always an imaginary door, balloon or ice cream cone, the weight and texture represented by counter-balance and muscular manipulation. When "Bip Goes Traveling," the person next to him is revealed by devices Marceau employs to create a positive area in the negative expanse of stage. Chaplin on the other hand works with tangibles—hat, flower, cane, folding Murphy bed—articles that are transformed into symbols in a dramatic relationship. In his hands, a prop is itself plus the entire dramatic potential of "prop to Chaplin." A malleable property such as the cane may appear as baseball bat, pool cue, nail file or sword; the impossible Murphy bed in *One O'Clock* becomes an image of all spiteful opposition. In every instance the real prop is his point of contact and departure—the "Dance of the Rolls" in *Gold Rush* or of the wrenches in *Modern Times* is a creative variation on something quite real and substantial employed symbolically toward abstraction and statement.

Rarely does Marceau cross from pantomime to mime. In "Bip and the Butterfly" he first communicates a mothlike presence by head movement that takes the rhythm of flutter and flight; this is pantomime. When he reaches for it, a different theory and new limitations come into play. The butterfly is not an illusion in his hand; it *is* his hand, and his hand is real, a prop that can accept a functional relationship. "Youth, Maturity, Old Age and Death," essentially a walk in place, is also mime. The body itself as a property related to dramatic time evokes the abstraction of a life.

One immediate notion about mime is that it has become a commodity without a purpose. Its development has been slight—some commercial work for a few people—and it may well become another total system devoted to keeping one healthy, off the streets, purifying the soul and making one live longer. To make mime an art form

In comparative terms:

The Pantomimist	The Mime
—closer to dance	—closer to drama
—usually masked and mute	—can speak and sing
—moves to music	—moves to act

Dealing with	*Using*
—"nothing there"	—tangible props
—he must communicate his prop	—he exhorts and manipulates their symbolism
—to tell the anecdote	—to comment on the story

Charmed audience	*Stimulated audience*
—the viewer guesses	—the viewer thinks
—"What does he have there?"	—"What does what he has there mean?"

separate from theatre—a nonintegrated element—only leads it to become a solo art form leaning on its pantomimic, not its mimetic, side.

Remembering the roots of our modern knowledge of mime—stemming from the work and study of Etienne Decroux—we see two paths to follow: not as I point out Marceau and Chaplin, rather Marceau and J. L. Barrault. Marceau continues as a solo performer and Barrault continues as a director-actor-producer of a theatre company. It is through the integration of mime derived from the work with Decroux that Barrault finds himself inside a theatrical situation.

And, if one studies the interviews and writings of Etienne Decroux carefully, and even tries to understand them with an interpreter—someone who studied with the *maitre* for a number of years—one finds that Decroux spoke in mimetic theory and performed in pantomimic form. The development of two rather different paths from the same classroom, Marceau-solo and Barrault-drama, demonstrates this paradox.

In my own work over the years from modern dance, through mime, to naturalistic theatre, to *commedia dell'arte* (radical theatre), and to the Epic Theatre of Bertolt Brecht, the understanding of the difference between pantomime and mime has proved to be of great value.

There is a need to explicate the similarities in the notion of mime derived from Decroux (and Paul Curtis) as I have defined it, and the notion of gestic acting or "gestus" in the theories and labors of Bertolt

Brecht. On its face, the idea of presenting representational illusions as in pantomime is not integrated in Epic theatre; it does, however, find a place with the improvisational work of those associated with Viola Spolin (who calls her pantomime "space objects"!). But here too, a small element of the total work of theatre has been extracted to create something called "improvisational theatre." It has been touted as if improvisation was the possession of a woman (and her followers) who spent some time saying whatever came to their mouths as quickly as possible.

There needs to be more clarification of interrelations or aberrations. In my forthcoming books, one on *commedia dell'arte* and another on storytelling for Epic Theatre, I will go into this subject.

Mime in the Streets

Jack Fincher

In 1971 Robert Shields developed his street mime and improvisa-
tions with passers-by in San Francisco's Union Square. Lorene
Yarnell, married to him in a public mimed ceremony, performs in
partnership with Shields; they appear in concerts, clubs, and have
been featured on television since 1976. This article appeared in
Saturday Review.

Sun-splashed Union Square, an island of lush lawns and manicured
flower beds in the concrete sea of the city. Hard-hats with their sand-
wiches, hippies with their dogs. Miniskirted office girls with paper
cups of yogurt lolling prettily on a greensward still warmly deep with
dew. Down below, in the thin, cold shadows of the tall palms, along
the low parapets that flank the wide sidewalk, the Stockton Street
regulars begin to gather for the noon show like a chattering window
of sparrows . . . .

And here he comes! Up the street in gleaming whiteface, his hair
a glossy, black Raggedy Ann mop, his eyes and mouth the harlequin's
gaping wounds of grease paint. He is wearing his black-and-white
drum major suit, marching at the head of his own imaginary parade,
"wheeling and spinning and throwing kisses," as E. B. White once
wrote, to the girls who wave gaily from the tall buildings.

> I get in the mood: Everything's a joke, the whole universe.
> Everyone's taking themselves so seriously. I'm saying life is
> a carnival! Ta-ta-da!

He vaults sprang in the middle of his sidewalk runway, does a running, sole-scorching slide the length of it and back, ending with a
complete flip that lands him on his feet facing a pair of very *macho*
cyclists.

> Their manner always said, "Look at this faggot." So I have
> to do a stunt to prove that I'm a gymnast.

Three businessmen approach. Robert joins them with a Groucho
Marx lope, his shaggy head floating eerily at their waists as they walk,
a secretary pecking a nonexistent typewriter, frantically place a Very
Important Call using his pulled-off shoe as the telephone. They shoot
self-conscious little smiles at each other, try to ignore him. He spies
an elderly woman shuffling along and flings himself prostrate before
her.

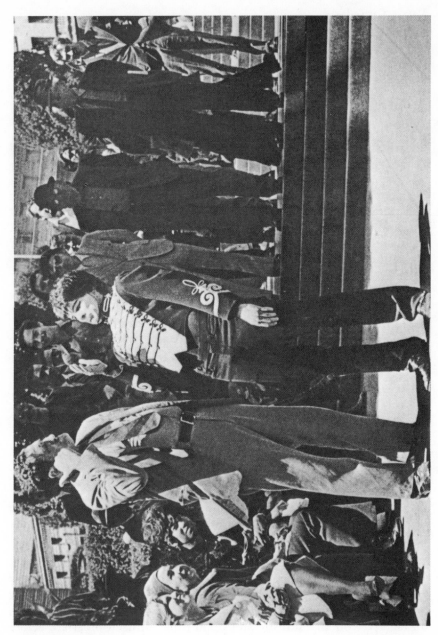

Figure 36. Robert Shields in Union Square, San Francisco. (Photo: Robert Scheu. Courtesy Robert Shields.)

Old people hang around parks just waiting for death. I think I help them.

He springs to his feet, falls in beside her with the same closed-off, uncertain shuffle. The crowd stirs.

If I'm a little cruel, I feel them saying, "Hey, man, that's no good!"

Abruptly he switches to an impassioned flamenco, heels tattooing the pavement, his hip against her hip, his eyes blazing madly into hers. For a few steps, it is touch and go; then her frozen old features melt into a delighted grin.

If I feel she's warm, I get right up next to her. She looks forbidding, but actually it's a mask—like mine.

He embraces her, gives her up forever at the corner with Chaplinesque poignancy. Poor Pierrot.

Robbed of his heart, Pierrot becomes The Mechanical Man. Eyes glazed, unblinking, face impassive as china, he glides about in interlocking little symmetries, arms chopping and jerking like levers run amok, wrists turning minutely on precision pivots, head thrusting and bobbing like a jack-in-the-box.

I do a little robot for a change of pace. It's more stylized than street mime.

A little girl shrinks away in terror and will not be won back. At the top of the steps, chance and the moment have thrown together a bewhiskered hippie and a sobersided executive. Robert is there in a wink. He puffs an illusory joint, pretends to pass it on to the hippie.

I use the joint image because it's the symbol of today. You know, are you gutsy enough to try this?

The hippie gravely takes a bogus hit, turns to Old Sobersides, thinks better of it, and returns it to Shields, who leaps across the sidewalk and lands on Eileen Von's ample lap. She shrieks with laughter, slaps the spectral grass from his hand, and, hugging him tightly, proclaims to the world that she will never let him go. The Toothpick Man beside her beams approval.

These people are my props. I know I can always depend on them.

Robert rises at last with the leaden dignity of a prelate, sprinkles them with holy water, and marries them.

A very cool black cat is watching malevolently. Robert runs to him, cuts from the cloth of the air a posture of the same murderous intensity. The black, mocked, rivets him with a gaze that chills your liver. Shields bounds away, takes refuge behind a forest of people, fires back indignant glances.

> I try to show him himself, and I fail. Sometimes, when you get bad vibes, you can put out your hand and say to them softly, "Listen, it's all in good humor, I'm just doing a job."

The black cat holds his ground, a squat, still monument to the threat of violence, but Robert and the crowd no longer care. He has discovered a young couple, stolen the girl, wooed her, lost her, mourned, and recovered before the man—his attention directed elsewhere by the thrust of an index finger—quite realizes what has happened. Shields then engages a smiling young Chinese in an orgy of bowing and is rewarded with a highly tangible kick in the pants. The crowd laughs; the young Chinese goes away quite pleased with himself.

> After all, it's really their show. The people's.

Robert silently barks down a dog—wow, they freak!—concludes with a left-handed scherzo on his invisible violin, and thus implored, the coins shower down. He sits, mopping his brow in an agony of exhaustion. He will drive his 5'7", 130-pound body like this for two hours. Why? Perhaps he has the answer for all of us.

> There's no barrier, no wall. No hype, no Hollywood. It's probably the most beautiful thing I'm ever going to do in my whole life. It's the purest kind of theatre.

*   *   *

Selected passages from *Mime in the Streets* by Robert Shields:

It's a process of changing mood; the act of putting on white face is like entering into a fantasy. I feel myself changing as the makeup goes on; by the time I'm done, I move differently, think differently, certainly act differently. In white face you become capable of fantasies that an ordinary face doesn't allow.

I understand masks. When I first started out in mime, I hid behind my makeup. The mask took all the credit or the blame. But I'm not afraid of people any more; I've performed successfully without white face. So now I understand masks. In Union Square I see women wearing at least as much makeup as I do when I'm performing. That's one kind of mask. I see frozen, cold, stiff faces, afraid to laugh or cry; that's another. So I put on my mask and go down to Union Square to see what I can do about theirs.

I'm very aware of people's feelings when I work in Union Square. I wasn't when I first started out, but I sure learned fast. I mirror them, show them how they look to others. People come up all the time and thank me for showing them outward mannerisms they didn't even know they had and should have gotten rid of. And a lot of these people haven't had anybody pay them any real loving attention in so long, they're frozen and stiff. When I run into somebody like that, I try to show them all the positive things about themselves, let them see themselves being applauded and appreciated by the crowd. I'm just the mirror.*

---

*The last paragraph is from an interview in Rolling Stone, June 8, 1972.

Epilogue: Anti-Mime

*If people have mouths, why don't they speak through
them instead of making signs?*
                                    —James Agate

*Would you not, Madame, look at a small effort of an
arrangement by some excellent individuals who wish
to please you? They are those who, by their steps,
their gestures, and their movements express all things
to one's eyes, and they call that* pantomimes. *I
trembled to employ that word to you, and there are
those of our court who would not forgive me.*

                              —Moliere,
                              *Les Amants
                              Magnifiques*

*Let wisdom and books go hang
And all this endless care.
Stand by the actor's side
Or sit in the jester's chair.
Spend all your time with the mimes—
Play with all their childish toys—
Nothing is honoured now
But jesting and laughter and noise.
Let wisdom's erstwhile noble rage
Be ceded to the mimic stage.*
                                    —Prodromos

*The comic part of the English Pantomimes being
duller than anything before shown on the stage could
only be set off by the superlative dullness of the serious
portion, in which the gods and goddesses were so
insufferably tedious, that Harlequin was always a
relief from still worse company.*
                              —Henry Fielding

216

E VERY ART HAS had its detractors, not so much of the art form as of individual practitioners.

But mime has its detractors of both form and practice, from antiquity and Prodromos's "Let wisdom's erstwhile noble rage/Be ceded to the mimic stage" to Woody Allen's half-serious miscomprehensions.

There seem to be two sorts of anti-mimes: those who dislike it outright and without qualification, and those who demonstrate ambivalence. Among the latter are Moliere and his ironic reluctance to use the word "pantomime" to a princess, and Paul Franck, himself a mime and producer of mime programs, who "never believed in it." Max Beerbohm's parody of English panto is matched by his statement that it is the one art form invented in England, as attractive as any art form the world has known—he even hints that it is a bit too good for the English public. The French poets and essayists who frequented Deburau's pantomimes at the Funambules wrote poems in its praise, and also called the scenarios puerile.

The following peppery remarks can give only pleasure to those of us whose love for mime is obstinately unalterable.

On a Panto Performance

Max Beerbohm

Sir Max Beerbohm (1872–1956) was a critic, essayist, caricaturist, and cartoonist whose wit and barbs epitomized the Gay Nineties. He succeeded George Bernard Shaw as theatre critic for Saturday Review.

> Full many Panto's truly there have been
> But this the best of all is, I do ween.
> And Mr. Collins has himself surpass'd*
> In Ali Baba and the Forty Thieves.
> And yet, somehow (to say so me it grieves!)
> I can't with truth declare I much enjoyed it—
> But don't suppose I mean *you* should avoid it!
> The fault's my *own* and, for that reason very,
> I'd best *own* up and bid you all be merry!
> If I myself don't like this Pantomime,
> Live and let live, boys! —it is all the same!
> To Drury Old, I'm certain, when you go, you—

BUT I HAVE written quite enough to show you, reader, how fearfully I have been haunted by the rhyming iambics in 'Ali Baba' at Drury Lane, and in 'Dick Whittington' at the Adelphi. In point of rhythm my lines are perhaps superior to theirs, but I think I have managed to suggest the kind of order in which the words come tripping, and also the level of humour and sense above which they seldom rise.

---

*A leading producer of pantomimes. —ED.

The Great Mimes
No Longer Believe in Their Art
Marc Blanquet

Marc Blanquet's piece appeared as a news story, and I've absolutely no information on him. He's not in the mime world so I assumed he was a news reporter.

MUSIC HALL IS TRIUMPHANT, cinema is King, operetta has regained its former popularity, and the success of these three forms is rather easily explained. Now, there are many foreigners in Paris, whose imperfect grasp of our language bars their attendance at our playhouses, to the benefit of variety shows, operettas, revues, and films. Why not revive that other international theatrical form, the pantomime?

Accessible to all, the art of Deburau might finally achieve, thanks to our gracious guests, the renascence which was lately much talked of, and which M. Paul Franck tried a few years ago on the stage of the Olympia.

"I don't venture to believe it," says M. Georges Wague. "Modern pantomime every day sees its own success increasing," declared the illustrious mime. "The cinema, is it anything else but a new form of mime? It triumphs everywhere, and certain films along the Boulevard have careers envied by a good number of dramatic authors. But in spite of that, and I even say *because* of that, I scarcely believe in a possible rebirth of pantomime. The variety of settings enjoyed by films offers too many advantages for the stage to contend with. And I tell you, I regret it."

"No, I think not," we are told by M. Paul Franck, who was a great mime and now is director of the music hall on the Boulevard des Capucines. "I think not, and I do not shrink from adding: I never thought so."

"???"

"You seem surprised? I assure you, I never believed in pantomime. I tried to but never succeeded. No, pantomime is incomplete and no one could any longer put up with it. My attempts with Séverin finally convinced me. It's over—well over—let's not talk about it."

Not talk about it! What would you say to that, Gaspard? And you, Charles Deburau?

219

A Little Louder, Please
Woody Allen

Woody Allen (b. 1935) has written television comedy, screen-plays, and many pieces for national magazines; he has acted in and directed films, and has received many awards.

UNDERSTAND YOU ARE dealing with a man who knocked off "Finnegan's Wake" on the roller coaster at Coney Island, penetrating the abstruse Joycean arcana with ease, despite enough violent lurching to shake loose my silver fillings. Understand also that I am among the select few who spotted instantly in the Museum of Modern Art's impacted Buick that precise interplay of nuance and shading that Odilon Redon could have achieved had he forsaken the delicate ambiguity of pastels and worked with a car press. Also, laddies, as one whose spate of insights first placed "Godot" in proper perspective for the many confused playgoers who milled sluggishly in the lobby during intermission, miffed at ponying up scalper's money for argle-bargle bereft of one up-tune or a single spangled bimbo, I would have to say my rapport with the seven livelies is pretty solid. Add to this the fact that eight radios conducted simultaneously at Town Hall killed me, and I still occasionally sit in with my own Philco, after hours, in a Harlem basement where we blow some late weather and news, and where once a laconic field hand named Jess, who had never studied in his life, played the closing Dow-Jones averages with great feeling. Real Soul stuff. Finally, to lock my case up tight, note that mime is a stock visage at happenings and underground-movie premieres, and that I am a frequent contributor to *Sight and Stream*, a cerebral quarterly dedicated to advanced concepts in cinema and fresh-water fishing. If these are not credentials enough to tag me Joe Sensitive, then, brother, I give up. And yet, with this much perception dripping from me, like maple syrup off waffles, I was reminded recently that I possess an Achilles' heel culturewise that runs up my leg to the back of my neck.

It began one day last January when I was standing in McGinnis's Bar on Broadway, engulfing a slab of the world's richest cheesecake and suffering the guilty, cholesterolish hallucination that I could hear my aorta congealing into a hockey puck. Standing next to me was a nerve-shattering blonde, who waxed and waned under a black chemise with enough provocation to induce lycanthropy in a Boy Scout. For the previous fifteen minutes, my "pass the relish" had been the central theme of our relationship, despite several attempts on my part to generate a little action. As it was, she *had* passed the relish, and I was forced to ladle a small amount on my cheesecake as witness to the integrity of my request.

"I understand egg futures are up," I ventured finally, feigning the insouciance of a man who merged corporations as a sideline. Unaware that her stevedore boy friend had entered, with Laurel and Hardy timing, and was standing right behind me, I gave her a lean, hungry look and can remember cracking wise about Krafft-Ebing just before losing consciousness. The next thing I recall was running down the street to avoid the ire of what appeared to be a Sicilian cousin's club bent on avenging the girl's honor. I sought refuge in the cool dark of a newsreel theatre, where a tour de force by Bugs Bunny and three Librium restored my nervous system to its usual timbre. The main feature came on and turned out to be a travelogue on the New Guinea bush— a topic rivalling Moss Formations and How Penguins Live for my attention span. "Throwbacks," droned the narrator, "living today not a whit differently from man millions of years ago, slay the wild boar [whose standard of living didn't appear to be up perceptibly, either] and sit around the fire at night acting out the day's kill in pantomime." Pantomime. It hit me with sinus-clearing clarity. Here was a chink in my cultural armor—the only chink, to be sure, but one that has plagued me ever since childhood, when a dumb-show production of Gogol's "The Overcoat" eluded my grasp entirely and had me convinced I was simply watching fourteen Russians doing calisthenics. Always, pantomime was a mystery to me—one that I chose to forget about because of the embarrassment it caused me. But here was that failing again and, to my chagrin, just as bad as ever. I did not understand the frenetic gesticulations of the leading New Guinea aborigine any more than I have ever understood Marcel Marceau in any of those little skits that fill multitudes with such unbounded adulation. I writhed in my seat as the amateur jungle thespian mutely titillated his fellow-primitives, finally garnering hefty mitt with money notices from the tribal elders, and then I slunk, dejected, from the theatre.

At home that evening, I became obsessed with my shortcoming. It was cruelly true: despite my canine celerity in other areas of artistic endeavor, all that was needed was one evening of mime to limn me clearly as Markham's hoe man—stolid, stunned, and brother to the ox in spades. I began to rage impotently, but the back of my thigh tightened and I was forced to sit. After all, I reasoned, what more elemental form of communication is there? Why was this universal art form patent in meaning to all but me? I tried raging impotently again, and this time brought it off, but mime is a quiet neighborhood, and several minutes later two red-necked spokesmen for the Nineteenth

Precinct dropped by to inform me that raging impotently could mean
a five-hundred-dollar fine, six months' imprisonment, or both. I
thanked them and made a beeline for the sheets, where my struggle to
sleep off my monstrous imperfection resulted in eight hours of noctur-
nal anxiety I wouldn't wish on Macbeth.

A further bone-chilling example of my mimetic shortcoming ma-
terialized only a few weeks later, when two free tickets to the theatre
turned up at my door—the result of my correctly identifying the singing voice of Mama Yancey on a radio program a fortnight prior. First
prize was a Bentley, and in my excitement to get my call in to the
disc jockey promptly I had bolted naked from the tub. Seizing the
telephone with one wet hand while attempting to turn off the radio
with the other, I ricocheted off the ceiling, while lights dimmed for
miles around, as they did when Lepke got the chair. My second orbit
around the chandelier was interrupted by the open drawer of a Louis
Quinze desk, which I met head on, catching an ormulu mount across
the mouth. A florid insignia on my face, which now looked as if it had
been stamped by a rococo cookie cutter, plus a knot on my head the
size of an auk egg, affected my lucidity, causing me to place second
to Mrs. Sleet Mazursky, and, scotching my dreams of the Bentley,
I settled for a pair of freebees to an evening of off-Broadway theatrics.
That a famed international pantomimist was on the bill cooled my
ardor to the temperature of a polar cap, but I decided to attend. I was
unable to get a date on only six weeks' notice, so I used the extra
ticket to tip my window-washer, Lars, a lethargic menial with all the
sensitivity of the Berlin Wall. At first he thought the little orange
pasteboard was edible, but when I explained that it was good for an
evening of pantomime—one of the only spectator events outside of a
fire that he could hope to understand—he thanked me profusely.

On the night of the performance, the two of us—I in my opera cape
and Lars with his pail—split with aplomb from the confines of a
Checker cab and, entering the theatre, strode imperiously to our seats,
where I studied the program and learned, with some nervousness,
that the curtain-raiser was a little silent entertainment entitled ''Going to a Picnic.'' It began when a wisp of a man walked onstage in
kitchen-white makeup and a tight black leotard. Standard picnic dress
—I wore it myself to a picnic in Central Park last year, and, with the
exception of a few adolescent malcontents who took it as a signal to
re-edit my salients, it went unnoticed. The mime now proceeded to
spread a picnic blanket, and, instantly, my old confusion set in. He
was either spreading a picnic blanket or milking a small goat. Next, he
elaborately removed his shoes, except I'm not positive that they were

his shoes, because he drank one of them and mailed the other to Pittsburgh. I say "Pittsburgh," but actually it is hard to mime the concept of Pittsburgh, and as I look back on it, I now think what he was miming was not Pittsburgh at all but a man driving a golf cart through a revolving door—or possibly two men dismantling a printing press. How that pertains to a picnic escapes me. The pantomimist then began sorting an invisible collection of rectangular objects, undoubtedly heavy, like a complete set of the Encyclopedia Britannica, which I suspect he was removing from the picnic basket, although from the way he held them they could also have been the Budapest String Quartet, bound and gagged.

By this time, to the surprise of those sitting next to me, I found myself trying, as usual, to help the mime clarify the details of his scene by guessing aloud exactly what he was doing. "Pillow . . . big pillow. Cushion? *Looks* like cushion . . ." This well-meaning participation often upsets the true lovers of silent theatre, and I have noticed a tendency on such occasions for those sitting next to me to express uneasiness in various forms, ranging from significant throat-clearings to a lion's paw swipe on the back of the head, which I once received from a member of a Manhasset housewives' theatre party. On this occasion, a dowager resembling Ichabod Crane snapped her lorgnette quirtlike across my knuckles, with the admonition "Cool it, Stud." Then, warming to me, she explained, with the patiently slow enunciation of one addressing a shell-shocked infantryman, that the mime was now dealing humorously with the various elements that traditionally confound the picnic-goer—ants, rain, and the always-good-for-a-laugh forgotten bottle opener. Temporarily enlightened, I rocked with laughter at the notion of a man harassed by the absence of a bottle opener, and marvelled at its limitless possibilities.

Finally, the mime began blowing glass. Either blowing glass or tattooing the student body of Northwestern University. It seemed like the student body of Northwestern University, but it could have been the men's choir—or a diathermy machine—or any large, extinct quadruped, often amphibious and usually herbivorous, the fossilized remains of which have been found as far north as the Arctic. By now, the audience was doubled up with laughter over the hi-jinx on the stage. Even the obtuse Lars was wiping tears of joy from his face with his squeegee. But for me it was hopeless; the more I tried, the less I understood. A defeated weariness stole over me, and I slipped off my loafers and called it a day. The next thing I knew, a couple of charwomen at work in the balcony were batting around the pros and cons of bursitis. Gathering my senses by the dim glow of the theatre work light, I straightened my tie and departed for Riker's, where a hamburger and a chocolate malted gave me no trouble whatever as to their meaning, and for the first time that evening I threw off my guilty burden. To this day, I remain uncomplete culturally, but I'm working on it. If you ever see an aesthete at a pantomime squinting, writhing, and muttering to himself, come up and say hello—but catch me early in the performance: I don't like to be bothered once I'm asleep.

Sources and Permissions

Acknowledgments and permissions on these pages constitute an extension of the copyright page in the front of this book.

"To Talk of Mime . . ." by Dominique Bourquin, from *Mimes Suisses, Un Aperçu*, Olivier Blanchard, editor, Guemligen, Switzerland: Zytglogge Verlag, 1975. Translated by B.R. Reprinted by permission of the author.

"On Pantomime" by Lucian, from *The Works of Lucian of Somosata*, translated by H. W. Fowler and F. G. Fowler and published by Oxford University Press (1949), Volume II pp. 249–261. Reprinted by permission of the publisher.

"Pylades and Bathyllus" by John Weaver from his *The History of Mimes and Pantomimes*, London: 1728, pp. 7–10.

"A Roman Premiere" is excerpted from the chapter "De la saltation chez les Romains," in *Le Geste* by Charles Hacks, Paris, 1892. Translated by B.R.

"Two Miracle Plays," anonymous, from *The Miracle Play in England* by Sydney W. Clarke, London, n.d.

Excerpts from "Etude sur la pantomime" by Paul Hippeau was published in *Pantomimes de Gaspard et Ch. Deburau*, edited by Emile Goby, Paris: Dentu, 1889, pp. xvi–xvii. Translated by B.R.

"The Italian Theatre" by Evaristo Gherardi is excerpted from his "The Preface to *Le Théâtre Italien*" as reprinted in *The Mask*, Volume 3, No. 10–12, April 1911, p. 169.

Elizabethan Dumb Shows: *Gorboduc* by Thomas Norton and Thomas Sackville, in *Early English Classical Tragedies*, John W. Cunliffe, editor, Oxford, 1912. *Hamlet* by William Shakespeare, in *The Works of William Shakespeare*, London: Ward Lock and Co., n.d. *Herod and Antipater* from *The True Tragedy of Herod and Antipater* by Gervase Markham and William Sampson, in *The Elizabethan Dumb Show* by Dieter Mehl, Cambridge: Harvard University Press, 1966.

"Some Symbolic Actions" by Cecilia Sieu-Ling Zung is excerpted from *Secrets of the Chinese Drama*, New York: Benjamin Blom, Inc., 1964. First published 1937. Reprinted by permission of the author.

"On the Mimique of the Noh" by Zeami is excerpted from *La Tradition Secrète du Nô*; pp. 83, 116, 117. Edited and translated into French by René Sieffert. © Unesco 1960. Reproduced by permission of Unesco. Translated by B.R.

"Notes on Indian Dramatic Technique" by Ananda Coomaraswamy is excerpted from his article in *The Mask*, Volume VI, No. 2, October 1913, pp. 123–128.

"Rich's Miming" is excerpted from *A History of Pantomime* by R. J. Broadbent. New York: Citadel Press, 1965; first published 1901.

"Ballet Pantomime" is excerpted from *Letters on Dancing and Ballets* by Jean Georges Noverre, translated by Cyril W. Beaumont. New York: Dance Horizons, Inc., 1966; from the revised and enlarged edition published at St. Petersburg, 1803. Reprinted by permission of Dance Horizons, Inc.

"A Pantomime Audience" by Jonathan Swift is taken from *Pantomimes for Stage and Study* by T. Earl Pardoe. New York: Benjamin Blom, Inc., 1971, pp. 44–45. Reprinted by Arno Press, Inc., 1976.

"Glaskull, the Edinburgh Butcher" is taken from *La Musique et la pantomime* by Paul Hugounet. Paris: Ernest Kolb, 1892; pp. 143–145. Translated by B.R.

"Deburau-Pierrot" is excerpted from *Mes Souvenirs* by Theodore de Banville. Paris: Bibliotheque Charpentier, 1911?; pp. 215–223. Translated by B.R.

"How to Listen to a Pantomime" by Horace Bertin, from *Les Soirées Funambulesques* by Felix Larcher and Paul Hugounet. Paris: Ernest Kolb, 1891. Translated by B.R.

"Souvenirs of a Mime" by Raoul de Najac is excerpted from his *Souvenirs d'un Mime*. Paris: Emile Paul, 1909. Translated by B.R.

"Pierrot Yesterday and Today" by Paul Margueritte is excerpted from *Mimes et Pierrots* by Paul Hugounet. Paris: Librairie Fischbacher, 33 rue de Seine, 75006 Paris, 1889. Reprinted by permission of the publisher. Translated by B.R.

"The Last of the Pierrots," excerpts from an interview with Séverin by Barrett H. Clark in *The Drama*, Volume 13, Nos. 11–12, August-September 1923.

"Grimaldi" is excerpted from *Popular Entertainments Through the Ages* by Samuel McKechnie, pp. 108–109. New York: 1931. Reprinted by Benjamin Blom, Inc., 1969. Distributed by Arno Press, Inc.

"The Hanlon-Lees Go To America" is excerpted from *Mime et Pierrots* by Paul Hugounet, pp. 198–200. Paris: Librairie Fischbacher, 33 rue de Seine, 75006 Paris. 1889. Reprinted by permission of the publisher. Translated by B.R.

"Dan Leno" is excerpted from *Cent Ans de Music Hall* by Jacques Charles. Paris: Editions Jeheber, 1956; pp. 73–74. Translated by B.R.

"The Pantomime Theatre of Tivoli Gardens" was written for this anthology by Ronald Smith Wilson.

"On Pantomime" is excerpted from *Theory of Theatrical Dancing* by Carlo Blasis; pp. 73–83. London: Frederick Verinder, 1888.

"Les Resources de L'art Muet" by Georges Wague appeared in *Excelsior*, Paris, July 9, 1933. Translated by B.R.

"Music Halls" by Colette is excerpted with the permission of Farrar, Straus & Giroux, Inc. from *Earthly Paradise* by Colette, an autobiography drawn from her lifetime writings by Robert Phelps, translated from the French by Herma Briffault, translation copyright © 1966 by Farrar, Straus & Giroux, Inc. Selections from "Bella-Vista" from *The Tender Shoot* by Colette, translated by Antonia White, copyright © 1958 by Martin Secker & Warburg and reprinted by permission of the publishers.

"The Cinema According to Max Linder" is excerpted from *Max Linder* by Charles Ford. Paris: Editions Seghers (Cinema d'aujourdhui #38 directed by Pierre Lherminier), 1966. Translated by B.R. Reprinted by permission of the publisher.

"Each Art Has Its Own Territory" by Ettienne Decroux is excerpted from "The Pretensions of Pantomime," *In Search of Theatre* by Eric Bentley. Copyright © 1950, 1953 by Eric Bentley. Reprinted by permission of Atheneum Publishers.

"Dramatic Art and the Mime" by Jean-Louis Barrault, from *Opera, Ballet, Music Hall,* International Theatre Institute publication III, UNESCO, 1953. Reprinted by permission of the publisher.

"The Mime and the Dancer" by Serge Lifar, from *Opera, Ballet, Music Hall,* International Theatre Institute publication III, UNESCO, 1953. Reprinted by permission of the publisher.

"Life's a Lark" by Grock is excerpted from the book of the same name. New York, 1931. Reprinted by Benjamin Blom, Inc., 1969. Distributed by Arno Press, Inc.

"The Mastery of Movement" by Rudolf Laban from the book of the same name. London: Macdonald and Evans, Ltd., 3d ed. 1971. Reprinted by permission of the publisher.

"My Sense of Drama" is excerpted from an interview with Charlie Chaplin by Richard Meryman for *Life* magazine. © 1967 Time Inc. Used with permission.

"My Wonderful World of Slapstick" by Buster Keaton is excerpted from the book of the same name. Copyright © 1960 by Buster Keaton and Charles Samuels. Reprinted by permission of Doubleday & Company, Inc.

"My World of Comedy" is excerpted from *Harold Lloyd's World of Comedy* by William Cahn. New York: Duell, Sloan and Pierce, 1964. Reprinted by permission of Rhoda Cahn.

"Mr. Laurel and Mr. Hardy" is excerpted from *Mr. Laurel and Mr. Hardy* by John McCabe. Copyright © by John McCabe. Reprinted by permission of Doubleday & Company, Inc.

"Bert Williams, Everybody" is excerpted from *Nobody, the Story of Bert Williams* by Ann Charters. New York: Macmillan Company, 1970. Copyright © 1970 by Ann Charters. Reprinted by permission of the publisher.

"Mime is a Lonely Art" is taken from *Angna Enters: On Mime.* Copyright © 1965 by Angna Enters. Reprinted by permission of Wesleyan University Press.

"Random Remarks" by Charles Weidman is taken from *The Dance Has Many Faces,* Walter Sorell, editor. New York: World Publishing Co., 1951. Reprinted by permission of Walter Sorell.

"I'll Tell All" by Red Skelton is excerpted from the *Milwaukee Journal*, December 8–12, 1941.

"The Adventure of Silence" by Marcel Marceau is excerpted from *Marcel Marceau ou L'aventure du Silence,* interview by Guy and Jeanne Verriest-Lefert, Paris: Desclee de Brouwer, 1974. Translated by B.R. and revised by Marcel Marceau. Reprinted by permission of Marcel Marceau.

"Mime, Movement, Theatre" by Jacques Lecoq was translated by Kat Foley and Julia Devlin and appeared in *yale/theatre* (now *Theater*) IV, #1, Winter 1973. Reprinted by permission of *Theater*. Subsequent changes made by B.R. at the request of M. Lecoq.

"The Cinema According to Tati" is excerpted from *Jacques Tati* by Armand J. Cauliez. Paris: Editions Seghers (Cinema D'aujourd'hui #7 directed by Pierre Lherminier), 1962. Translated by B.R. Reprinted by permission of the publisher.

"Mime and 'Something else' " was prepared for this anthology and published courtesy of Pinok and Matho.

"Mime in Great Britain" by Clifford Williams, from *Opera, Ballet, Music Hall*, International Theatre Institute publication III, UNESCO, 1953. Reprinted by permission of the publisher.

"Russian Clown" is excerpted from *Russian Clown* by Oleg Popov. © 1967 Novosti and Opera Mundi. London: Macdonald and Jane's Publishers Ltd., 1970. Translated by Marion Koenig. Reprinted by permission of the publisher and Opera Mundi.

"Movement Theatre" by Henryk Tomaszewski is excerpted from *Tomaszewski's Mime Theatre* by Andrzej Hausbrandt. Warsaw: Interpress Publishers, 1975. Reprinted by permission of the publisher.

"The Art of Dario Fo" is excerpted from *Mistero Buffo* by Dario Fo. Verona: Bertani Editore, 1973. Translated by B.R. Reprinted by permission of the publisher.

"The Fools, or a Strange Dream of a Clown" by Ladislav Fialka is the program note for the production "The Fools." Reprinted courtesy of Mr. Fialka.

"A Topsy-Turba World" by Kuster Beaton was prepared for this anthology by the editor.

"Dimitri, Clown" is excerpted from *Dimitri Album* by Dimitri. Bern: Benteli Verlag, 1973. Reprinted by permission of the publisher.

"Mask, Mime, and Mummenschanz" is excerpted from an interview by Bari Rolfe. *Mime Journal*, Number Two, Thomas Leabhart, editor. Published by the University of Arkansas, Fayetteville, 1975. Reprinted by arrangement with Mr. Leabhart.

"Zen Mime" by Mamako Yoneyama is taken from her program notes and commentary. Reprinted by permission of Mamako Yoneyama.

"How Sweet It Is . . ." by Lotte Goslar was specially written for this anthology.

"Mime in the Medium" by Dick Van Dyke was prepared for this anthology and printed here courtesy of Mr. Van Dyke, 1979.

"American Mime" by Paul J. Curtis was prepared for this anthology and printed here courtesy of Mr. Curtis, 1979.

"Commedia and the Actor" by Carlo Mazzone-Clementi (excerpts) first published in *The Drama Review*, Vol. 18, no. 1, T61. © 1974 by *The Drama Review*. Reprinted by permission. All Rights Reserved.

"Price of Folly" by Antonin Hodek is taken from his program notes. Reprinted by permission of Mr. Hodek.

"Mime: Self-Imposed Silence" is excerpted from an article by Samuel Avital that appeared in *The Movement*, June 1975 and *Le Centre du Silence Work Book*, 2d ed., 1977. Reprinted with permission from the *Movement Newspaper*, copyright 1975.

"Bernard Bragg and the National Theatre of the Deaf" by Helen Powers is excerpted from *Signs of Silence* by Helen Powers. New York: Dodd Mead & Company, 1972. Copyright © 1972 by Helen Powers. Reprinted by permission of the author and publisher.

"Method in Mime" by R. G. Davis was prepared for this anthology by Mr. Davis. Some of the material first appeared in *Tulane Drama Review*, June 1962, and *Players Magazine*, October-November 1972.

Selected Bibliography

THE FOLLOWING BIBLIOGRAPHY LISTINGS are in addition to those from which the anthology entries are taken (see Sources and Permissions). The references below deal mainly with history of mime and biographies of mimes. For a comprehensive bibliography, including films, periodicals, and scripts, consult the MIME DIRECTORY BIBLIOGRAPHY, 2d ed. 1978, edited by the present author and published by International Mimes and Pantomimists (see Prologue).

Agel, Genevieve. *Hulot parmi nous.* Paris: Editions du Cerf, 1955. In French.

Allen, P.S. "The Medieval Mimus." *Modern Philology* 7 (1910): 329–346.

Avery, Emmett L. "Entertainment on the English Stage 1700–1731." Thesis, University of Chicago, 1933.

Banville, Theodore de. "Theodore de Banville and the Hanlon-Lees Troupe." Translated by Richard Southern. *Theatre Notebook* 2 (1948): 70–75.

Barr, Charles. *Laurel and Hardy.* Berkeley and Los Angeles: University of California Press, 1968.

Barrault, Jean-Louis. *Memories for Tomorrow.* Translated by Jonathan Griffin. London: Thames and Hudson, 1974.

Beaumont, Cyril W. *The History of Harlequin.* New York: Benjamin Blom, Inc., 1926 and 1967.

Bieber, Margarete. *The History of Greek and Roman Theater.* Princeton, N.J.: Princeton University Press, 1961.

———. "Mima Saltatricula." *American Journal of Archeology* 43 (1939): 640–644.

Blesh, Rudi. *Keaton.* New York: MacMillan, 1966.

Carlson, Marvin. "The Golden Age of the Boulevard." *The Drama Review* 18 (1974): 25–33.

Champfleury. *Souvenirs des funambules.* Paris: Levy, 1859. In French.

Chaplin, Charles S. *My Autobiography.* New York: Pocket Books, 1966.

Cluzel, Magdeleine. *Mimes et poètes antiques.* Paris: Scorpion, 1957. In French.

Cunliffe, John W. "Italian Prototypes of the Masque and Dumb Show." *PMLA* 22 (1907): 140–156.

Davis, R.G. *The San Francisco Mime Troupe, The First Ten Years.* Palo Alto: Ramparts Press, 1975.

Decroux, Etienne. *Paroles sur le mime.* Paris: Gallimard, 1963. In French.

Despot, Adriane. "Jean Gaspard Deburau and the Pantomime at the Théâtre des Funambules." *Educational Theatre Journal* 27 (1975): 364–376.

Dickens, Charles. *Memoirs of Joseph Grimaldi.* Edited by Richard Findlater. New York: Stein and Day, 1968.

Disher, M. Willson. *Clowns and Pantomimes,* 1925. Reprint, New York: Benjamin Blom, Inc., 1968.

Dorcy, Jean. *The Mime.* New York: Robert Speller and Sons, 1961.

Duchartre, Pierre Louis. *The Italian Comedy.* New York: Dover, 1965.

Enters, Angna. *Artist's Life.* New York: Coward McCann, 1958.

———. *On Mime.* Middletown, Conn. Wesleyan University Press, 1965.

———. *Silly Girl.* Boston: Houghton, 1944.

Ericksen, Svend. "The Commedia dell'Arte is Still Alive in Danish Pantomime."
Opera, Ballet, Music Hall, International Theatre Publication III, 1953.
Everson, William K. The Films of Laurel and Hardy. New York: Cadillac, 1967.
Fields, W. C. W. C. Fields By Himself: His Intended Autobiography. Englewood Cliffs,
N.J.: Prentice Hall, 1973.
Findlater, Richard. Grimaldi, King of Clowns. New York: Stein and Day, 1968.
Fitzgerald, Percy H. "Rich and the Pantomimes." A New History of the English Stage.
2 vols. London: Tinsley, 1882.
Gibbs, Lloyd G. A History of the Development of the Dumb Show as a Dramatic
Convention. Los Angeles: University of Southern California Press, 1959.
Gillar, Jaroslav and Dana Pasekova. Ladislav Fialka and the Pantomime. Prague:
Orbis, 1971.
Goby, Emile, ed. Pantomimes de Gaspard et Ch. Deburau. Paris: Dentu, 1889. In
French.
Huston, Hollis. "The Zen Mime of Mamako." Educational Theatre Journal 12 (1976):
355–362.
Hybner, Boris. "Boris Hybner Reviews His Mime." Translated by Paul Wilson. Mime
Journal, nos. 3 and 4 (1976), pp. 14–28.
Kerr, Walter. The Silent Clowns. New York: Knopf, 1975.
Kozik, Francis. The Great Deburau. New York: Farrar and Rinehart, 1940.
Lawson, Joan. "Gorboduc." The Dancing Times, November 1918: 65–67.
Leabhart, Thomas. "An Interview With Decroux." Mime Journal, no. 1 (1974),
pp. 26–37.
Lebel, Jean Patrick. Buster Keaton. Translated by P. D. Stovin. London and New York:
Barnes, 1967.
Leno, Dan. Dan Leno Hys Booke. Edited by John Duncan. London: Hugh Evelyn,
Ltd., 1968.
Lesclide, Richard. Mémoires et pantomimes des frères Hanlon-Lees. Paris: Reverchon
et Vollet, 1880.
Littlewood, S. R. The Story of Pierrot. London: Herbert and Daniel, 1911.
Lorelle, Yves. L'Expression Corporelle du mime sacré au mime de théâtre. Paris: La
Renaissance du Livre, 1974. In French.
Mayer, David III. Harlequin in His Element. Cambridge: Harvard University Press,
1969.
Mic, Constant. La Commedia dell'Arte, 1914. Paris: Pleïade, 1927. In French.
Nicoll, Allardyce. Masks, Mimes and Miracles. New York: Cooper Square Pub., 1931
and 1963.
———. The World of Harlequin. Cambridge, England: Cambridge University Press,
1963.
Niklaus, Thelma. Harlequin, or the Rise and Fall of a Bergamask Rogue. New York:
Braziller, 1956.
Orme, Frederic. "Charles Weidman, The Master Mime." American Dancer 12
(1938): 11.
Pasekova, Dana. "Boleslav Polivka, an Appreciation of Pepe." Translated by Paul
Wilson. Mime Journal, nos. 3 and 4 (1976), pp. 56–69.
Rémy, Tristan. Georges Wague, Mime de la Belle Epoque. Paris: Girard, 1964. In
French.
Richards, Sandra L. "He Left Them Laughing." San Francisco Theatre Magazine,
vol. 1, no. 3, Summer 1978.
Robinson, David. Buster Keaton. Bloomington, Ind.: Indiana University Press, 1969.

Rolfe, Bari. "Mime in America, A Survey." *Mime Journal*, no. 1 (1974), pp. 2–12.
———. "Queens of Mime." *Dance Magazine* 50 (1976): 68–73.
Scott, Virginia. "The Infancy of English Pantomime: 1716–1728." *Educational Theatre Journal* 24 (1972): 125–138.
Séverin. *L'Homme blanc.* Paris: Plon, 1929. In French.
Simon, Karl Gunter. *Samy Molcho, Meister der Pantomime.* Hanover: Fredrich, 1965. In German.
Svehla, Jaroslav. "Deburau—The Immortal Pierrot." *Mime Journal*, no. 5 (1977), pp. 7–43.
Towsen, John. *Clowns.* New York: Hawthorn, 1976.
Turba, Ctibor. "Ctibor Turba Comments on Photographs of His Mime Work." Translated by Paul Wilson. *Mime Journal*, nos. 3 and 4 (1976), pp. 30–54.
Weaver, John. *The History of the Mimes and Pantomimes.* London: J. Roberts, 1728.
Wilson, A. E. *King Panto* (English ed. *Christmas Pantomime*, 1934). New York: Dutton, 1935.
Winter, Marian Hannah. *The Theatre of Marvels.* Translated by Charles Meldon. New York: Benjamin Blom, Inc., 1961.